ISLAM IS . . .

ISLAM IS . . .

An Experience of Dialogue and Devotion

New and Revised Edition

∾

Mary Margaret Funk, OSB

Lantern Books • New York
A Division of Booklight Inc.

2003, 2008
Lantern Books
A Division of Booklight Inc.
128 Second Place, Brooklyn, NY 11231

Printed in the United States of America.

Library of Congress Cataloging-in-Publication Data

Funk, Mary Margaret.
Islam is : an experience of dialogue and devotion / Mary
Margaret Funk--New Expanded ed.
p. cm.
Includes bibliographical references
ISBN-13: 978-1-59056-125-6 (alk. paper)
ISBN-10: 1-59056-125-2 (alk. paper)
1. Islam. 2. Islam—Essence, genius, nature. 3. Islam—Rela-
tions—Christianity. 4. Christianity and other religions—Islam.
I. Title
BP161.3.F86 2008
297—dc22
                                                      2008004714

ACKNOWLEDGMENTS

I would like to acknowledge the following for their help on this book: Martin Rowe, Gene Gollogly, Sarah Gallogly, Dr. Shahid Athar, Dr. John Borelli, Bishop Michael L. Fitzgerald, Dr. Sayyid M. Syeed, Katie Funk, Colleen Mathews, Mary Sue Freiberger, OSB, Carol Falkner, OSB, and my community, Sharon Richardt, DC, William Skudlarek, OSB, and the MID Board, the Serra Club of Indianapolis, Jane Owens and Friends of Benedict, Patrick Hart, OCSO, Trace Murphy, Judith Cebula, Kevin Funk, and Laura Klauberg.

CONTENTS

⌒

FOREWORD

⁀

MICHAEL L. FITZGERALD

I write these words at a time when the papers and the TV news bulletins are full of the assassination of Benazir Bhutto. Yet the papers here in Cairo also carry pictures of pilgrims returning joyfully from Mecca. Which offer us the true picture? Is Islam in essence a violent religion, or is it one that brings peacefully together people of different nations bound by a common faith? These questions are important, for Muslims form roughly one-fifth of the world's population, while Christians of all denominations would make up about one-third of the population. Relations between Christians and Muslims thus become an important factor for peace in the world.

It would have been possible to write a book entitled *Islam Is Not . . .* , countering the various accusations thrown against Islam: that it is legalistic, fatalistic, intolerant, discriminatory, and so on. There is always a need to rectify misunderstandings, to over-

come prejudices. In *Islam Is . . .* Sister Mary Margaret
Funk has adopted a positive approach, aiming to
provide a tool for understanding Islam. She is looking
at this religion from the outside, since it is not her own
faith, but she proceeds with a sympathy springing
from prayerful contact with Muslims.

The *Fatiha*, the opening *sura* or chapter of the
Qur'an, is an invocation which forms part of the
ritual prayer offered by Muslims. It addresses the
following words to God: *Guide us along the right
path*. Islam is indeed a path, a "way of life," which
the faithful Muslim strives to follow with the help of
God's guidance and in the light of the example of
Muhammad. Sister Meg gives considerable space in
this concise book to outline the life and experience of
the Prophet of Islam. It is always important to
remember the place that Muhammad occupies, not
only in the history of Islam, but also in the hearts of
Muslims. The book then goes on to treat of the five
"pillars" on which Islam rests, the fundamental
practices of witness, prayer, alms-giving, fasting, and
pilgrimage. Islam, of course, has enlarged these
foundations, developing a law (*shari'a*) that covers
every aspect of life. As Sister Meg points out, there is
little distinction in Islam between the religious and
the profane. Also, Islam has developed in the realm
of devotion, with Muslim scholars and sages writing
deeply on the spiritual life, and Sufi brotherhoods

providing additional forms of prayer and creating strong bonds of unity.

One of the insights shared in this book is that Islam owes much to its origins in Arabia. The experience of the desert has shaped a religious mentality. Yet it must be remembered that Islam has spread to many different parts of the world and has been able to adapt to different circumstances. This means that the "world of Islam" is marked by cultural differences. In other words, we may be able to say what *Islam Is* . . . ; but it would be more difficult to define what *Muslims Are.* . . . This, too, is important to bear in mind, for our meeting is not with a religion in the abstract, but with individual followers of that religion. We need to take care not to be blocked either by our lack of knowledge or by our expertise, so that we can encounter people as they really are. We may well meet Muslims who are struggling themselves with the phenomenon of violent fundamentalism, who are concerned about the role of women in society, and who are strong supporters of democracy—to mention only the three questions that Sister Meg raises at the conclusion of her book.

Islam Is . . . does not pretend to give the whole picture. It presents shots of some essential elements with a view to encouraging further discovery. The true meeting of people of different religions, of Christians and Muslims, is usually a long process. It is a

meeting of minds and hearts, sustained by faith in
God that, though differentiated, is nevertheless
shared. May this meeting take place more and more,
bringing peace to the hearts of individuals, and peace
to our world.

INTRODUCTION

Our Experience in Dialogue

⁓

JOHN BORELLI, PhD

It is a delight to be asked to update my introduction to Mary Margaret Funk's book, *Islam Is* . . . . She is a close friend, and someone whom I have admired for a very long time. Forty years ago, the American public was discovering Asian religions as numerous teachers of Buddhist, Hindu, and other spiritual traditions were establishing centers in significant numbers throughout the United States. Americans were increasingly curious about meditation as they began turning to Asian traditions for instruction. A handful of monastic women and men in the religious orders of the Benedictine family were taking note of this trend. Developing a positive approach, they responded in cooperation with teachers of Asian religious practices while recovering and modifying Christian contemplative practices that had suffered from neglect. Within a few years and in response to an invitation from

1

Catholic officials in Rome, they formed a network in
support of interreligious dialogue. Needless to say,
they became skilled practitioners of dialogue while
filling the critical need for teachers of Christian
contemplative practices.

Mary Margaret Funk, OSB, is prominent among
these Catholic men and women who emerged from
the interplay of contemplative practices and interreligious dialogue during the last decades of the twentieth
century. She is an expert in interreligious understanding and a skilled teacher of Christian contemplative practices. Her trilogy (*Thoughts Matter*, *Tools
Matter*, and *Humility Matters*) stands out as a product
of this widespread effort to recover and present a
tradition of Christian contemplation that was largely
lost to the life of the church. She also has gained from
her interaction with Buddhist and Hindu teachers in
sharpening the necessary skills Christian spiritual
directors need for teaching meditation today.

Sister Meg and I first met while she was the Executive Director of Monastic Interreligious Dialogue
(MID). Her primary experience in interreligious
dialogue followed from this work in supporting the
network of Catholic monastics dedicated to intermonastic dialogue, mainly with Buddhist, Hindu, and
Sufi "monastics," taking this latter term broadly.
While intermonastic dialogue is by no means closed to
those of us who are not monks and nuns, it has its

special character. Monastics—whether Buddhist, Catholic, Hindu, or other—are trained, or "formed," to live a routine of prayer, work, study, and service to others. Regardless of the differences they have as members of diverse religious traditions, they share certain experiences—rising early for prayer, holding regular meetings with a spiritual guide, using disciplines to effect spiritual growth, keeping routines of communal religious life, and so forth. Those of us who are not monastics are blessed to join these intermonastic exchanges, using the events as spiritual retreats; but we leave and go home to our families and the routines of life outside monastic environments. Intermonastic dialogues are especially attractive to us because the emphasis on spirituality is so critically important for successful interreligious dialogue, if one would measure success as growth in faith and the spiritual life.

Precisely as a monastic, as one skilled in spiritual techniques and interreligious dialogue, Sister Meg Funk was asked to join the Midwest Dialogue of Catholics and Muslims. This dialogue was one of three regional dialogues that I developed during my sixteen years on the staff of the U.S. Conference of Catholic Bishops (USCCB). The bishops' conference co-sponsored these dialogues with Islamic organizations and groups. While the model for this dialogue and the original idea to attempt them were my ideas,

I can take only a small fraction of the credit for their success.

The first Catholic bishop to serve as Episcopal Moderator for Interreligious Relations was, like Sister Meg, a Benedictine monastic: Joseph J. Gerry, OSB, bishop of the Catholic diocese of Portland, Maine. In the monastic spirit, once he had agreed to serve as interreligious moderator, he signed up for a summer course on Islam at the Pontifical Institute for Arabic and Islamic Studies in Rome. He demonstrated a willingness to learn. He also eagerly met with the board of Monastic Interreligious Dialogue to hear of their experiences and suggestions. He and I soon agreed that the monastics were indeed maintaining fruitful exchanges with Buddhists and some Hindu leaders across the country, and that we should leave most of that work to them. We decided to use our limited time and resources to promote dialogue with the Islamic community in the United States because, we felt, there were more practical consequences to building rapport between Catholics and Muslims in the United States with regard to a developing global situation. We reached this decision fully ten years before September 11, 2001.

In the early 1990s, Bishop Gerry and I invited Catholics and Muslims already active in Catholic–Muslim dialogue from all over the country to gather in Washington, DC. This took place with joint sponsorship of the American Muslim Council and the USCCB. Muslims and Catholics came from Los Angeles, Boston, Detroit, Houston, New York, and elsewhere. We had two meetings that were fruitful in establishing trust and rapport; however, we faced two principal difficulties in maintaining a national dialogue—time and money. Goodwill and hope were in abundance, but the costs of travel and the staff time necessary for such dialogues were a luxury for Islamic organizations. Their leadership wanted ongoing dialogue, but their priorities naturally required their attention for networking Muslim communities, advocating for their interests in the halls of the United States Government, maintaining communications with the news media, supporting local communities, and convening Muslims for community building projects. Setting funds aside for a national interreligious dialogue with the Catholic Church was beyond their scope and means.

After one of my new Muslim friends from the Washington, DC, area, Dr. Sayyid M. Syeed, relocated to Indianapolis, to serve as executive director of the Islamic Society of North America (ISNA), headquartered in the suburb of Plainfield, I began a series of visits to Indianapolis. My host was always the ecumenical/interreligious officer of the Archdiocese of Indianapolis, Father Thomas Murphy, pastor of old St. John's, the downtown parish. With him, we met

with Dr. Syeed and other Muslim leaders of the city
already in contact with the Catholic archdiocese.
Outstanding among these was Dr. Shahid Athar. His
leadership made the important difference. After three
exploratory visits, I proposed to Dr. Syeed and Dr.
Athar that ISNA and the USCCB co-sponsor an
annual conversation between Catholics and Muslims
in Indianapolis. Over time, the Christian and Muslim
planners and participants developed the model for a
regional dialogue. Bishop Gerry recommended a
Catholic bishop to serve as the Catholic co-chair who
would co-preside at meetings with Dr. Syeed. Staff
from the USCCB and ISNA planned the meeting; we
used local facilities and invited Catholics and Muslims
from cities within an easy commute of Indianapolis to
attend the meeting together.

Regional dialogues depended on support from
Catholic and Muslim leadership in the cities and
towns surrounding the meeting site. For Indianapolis,
this included Louisville, Toledo, St. Louis, Chicago,
Detroit, Milwaukee, Fort Wayne, South Bend, and
elsewhere. Usually the Catholic representative at a
regional dialogue was the diocesan ecumenical/inter-
religious officer; and usually, but not always, the
Muslim participant was the imam at a prominent
mosque in the territory of that diocese. The Catholic
and Muslim partners from a particular city or diocese
were already friends, having cooperated on a number

of local projects and initiatives. Regional dialogues also depended on good relations in the hosting environment so that Catholic and Muslim participants would feel supported by their communities at the site of the meeting. Finally, dialogue leaders identified scholars to do much of the work in presenting papers and preparing common statements. These arrangements required flexibility and openness.

The first meeting of the Midwest Dialogue of Catholics and Muslims took place in 1996. The following year, Sister Meg came to an evening program open to the public. By then, the members of the dialogue had decided that the topic for future meetings would be the expression "the word of God." We had begun in earnest in the second year, discussing Jesus Christ, who is the Word of God made flesh for Christians, and God's guidance in divine words, which Muslims believe is the Qur'an. We also started some intertextual work, providing exegesis of relevant passages of the New Testament and the Qur'an. By the third meeting, we wanted to compare how in each of our traditions the word of God is prayed, and I asked Sister Meg to speak on the practice of *lectio divina*—the attentive reading of scripture as a form of prayer. After her talk, which held our Muslim friends spellbound, as she drew from the depth of monastic tradition, Sister Meg became a regular participant in our dialogues. She participated eloquently and attentively at all subsequent meetings.

All our regional dialogues were retreats. Without this spiritual dimension, brought to a dialogue with breaks for regular prayer and with prayer in the meetings, the dialogues are lacking as interreligious dialogues. Catholics will attend Muslim prayers and Muslims attend a morning or evening prayer service specially prepared for the occasion. The Catholics also celebrate Eucharist each morning. Prayer assisted us as we addressed difficult contemporary issues.

It was in this environment of dialogue and prayer that Sister Meg grew in her knowledge of the faith and practices of Muslims. This volume, in many ways, is a product of the Midwest Dialogue and the other opportunities for interaction with Muslims that arose for her as a consequence of this dialogue and her work with Monastic Interreligious Dialogue. These Catholic–Muslim dialogues took place from 1996, through 2001, and beyond. The times always seemed difficult, even before 9/11, for dialogue between Christians and Muslims. Hostilities in the Middle East were always in the background, and during that period it seemed very difficult to bring Jews, Muslims, and Christians together in a public way. Yet, despite these and other difficulties, our dialogue proved both fruitful and necessary.

In a dialogue, participants listen more often than

they speak. Sometimes, a dialogue will issue a report or a statement; sometimes, individuals in a dialogue will write about the proceedings. A report, whether agreed upon word for word by all participants or prepared solely by an individual, is only a glimpse into what happens in a dialogue. Many times, I am asked for permission to record one of our dialogues, and I always turn down such a request. When a dialogue is recorded it ceases to be a dialogue and becomes a public event wherein everything said is put under careful scrutiny. People need to be at ease and to experience the trust of a group, to offer their thoughts, not quite formulated with accuracy, or to speak their minds. Sometimes we have to be candid with one another in dialogue. Candor is required for the sake of truth and charity, but it works differently within the confines of a dialogue from the public arena. Everyone needs to be honest, and simple honesty works best in public statements. Often topics are not simple, but complicated. Candor becomes a tool for understanding within the confines of dialogue.

Our Midwest dialogue demonstrated how two national sponsors could share costs. ISNA provided meeting space, and the USCCB took care of overnight rooms for the travelers. Meal costs are shared for the food that is provided by a Muslim caterer. The Catholics attend evening prayer with the Muslims and held a vespers afterward for the Muslims to attend. At times, the same space used by Muslims for prayer would be used by the Catholics for their daily Eucharist. Most participants absorbed the cost of travel since many came by car, and often traveled together. Expenses for the scholars were paid by the two sponsors. Sharing the cost of a dialogue is a necessary ingredient. Dialogues should not be bought but paid for. The fact that most participants are already skilled in Christian–Muslim relations insured that meetings go beyond introductory conversation. The Catholic and Muslim partners returned to their hometowns and cities with a renewed spirit of coop-eration for promoting relations at home.

In 1998, two years after the Midwest Dialogue began in Indianapolis, the Mid-Atlantic regional dialogue between the Islamic Circle of North America (ICNA) and the USCCB held its first meeting. ICNA is headquartered in Jamaica, Queens, New York. A Catholic bishop and a representative of ICNA co-chaired the sessions. After an initial meeting at a retreat house on Staten Island and the second meeting at St. Charles Seminary in Philadelphia, the dialogue settled into the routine of meeting at Immaculate Conception Center, a facility owned by the Diocese of Brooklyn and located in Queens. It provided overnight rooms and meeting space for very little cost. Some food was catered from an Islamic kitchen.

ICNA has its headquarters nearby. This dialogue focused on marriage and family. At the fourth meeting in March 2001, we spent one evening at the Islamic Center of Long Island in Westbury, New York. There, the participants attended evening prayer and then listened to two presentations. The following year we held a similar set of events at ICNA's headquarters. Holding a public event in the community that includes a meal is a way for the Muslim participants to share in the sponsorship of the cost of the dialogue.

A third regional dialogue was situated in Orange County, California, at the Center for Spiritual Development in the Diocese of Orange. It first met in 2000 with sponsorship shared between Sunni and Shiite Muslim leaders in Southern California. A Catholic bishop co-chaired with two Muslims, one Sunni and one Shiite, both serving as imams and directors of their Islamic center in the Orange County area. This group settled on the topic of surrender or obedience to God, and spirituality became the general subject of its first four meetings. For this dialogue, one evening was spent at either the Sunni or the Shiite center with evening prayer, a meal, and a public program. Presentations at the 2001 public program by Archbishop Alexander Brunett of Seattle and Dr. Muzammil Siddiqi were published in the March 29, 2001, issue of *Origins*, the documentary service of Catholic News Service. After completion of an agreed-upon set of

four meetings, the leadership of the dialogue
composed, circulated, and approved a common statement, *Friend and Not Adversaries: A Catholic–Muslim
Spiritual Journey*, completed in 2003 and posted on
the USCCB website (www.usccb.org/seia/friends.
shtml).

All three regional dialogues met annually, in a
retreat environment, over one or two days. Participants attended from Indianapolis, Detroit, Chicago,
St. Louis, Louisville, Cleveland, Toledo, Fort Wayne,
Lafayette, New York, Rockville Centre, Buffalo,
Newark, Trenton, Philadelphia, Harrisburg, Orange,
San Diego, Los Angeles, San Francisco, San Jose,
Sacramento, and Seattle. The model worked over the
period 1996 to 2003. This does not mean that the
model should continue. Different times may require
different models.

We are now in a different time after the second
Iraq war and the spread of global terrorism. Despite
these and other negative developments, there are positive signs, too. The interreligious legacy of Pope John
Paul II has provided a lasting memory for Catholics
and Muslims alike that they can cooperate together in
prayer and dialogue for the benefit of the whole of
humanity. In addition, in October 2007, an impressive
collection of Muslim scholars and leaders, organized
by Jordan's Royal Aal al-Bayt Institute for Islamic

Thought, issued "A Common Word between Us and You," a sophisticated, scripturally based invitation to Christian leaders for interreligious dialogue. This in many ways is the first widespread response by Muslims, based upon consensus, which is a critically important tool in their intellectual history, to the Second Vatican Council's invitation to dialogue contained in its *Declaration on the Relation of the Church to Non-Christian Religions (Nostra Aetate)*.

When the regional dialogues met, the first session was usually an opportunity to catch up on what had happened in the intervening year. It was the opportunity for friends to share their successes, failures, hopes, and fears. There would have been no point in us coming together as friends and interreligious companions unless we listened to what was truly troubling us. Thus, our meetings after September 11, 2001, were extremely profound and touched all participants at the deepest levels of friendship and trust. Gradually, each of the dialogues took time out from the schedule to address questions of religion, scripture, and violence. Afterward, our conversations became more probing and our insights more profound. As the war on terrorism unfolded, the intensity of our friendships and conversations increased.

These reflections by Sister Meg on our relationship in dialogue through the Midwest Dialogue constitute a lesson in growth. In that dialogue, we learned a great deal about the faith and practice of one another's religious tradition. We seemed especially blessed and touched by this experience of Catholic–Muslim dialogue. Sister Meg shows how dialogue is not an isolated activity but a spiritual practice. As we develop a Christian spirituality for interreligious dialogue, the testimonies of those involved in these dialogues and who also serve as spiritual guides will nurture us and give us insight.

PREFACE

This new revised edition of *Islam Is* . . . comes at a time when the dialogue between Muslims and Christians has proceeded with five years of daily contact because of world affairs. When I wrote the book in 2002, it was as a response to the events of September 11, 2001. From the perspective of 2008, we see what five years of war has brought upon our fragile world, and we can only hope that dialogue will some day replace violence as a solution to our problems.

This book is the fruit of dialogue among seasoned participants of many interfaith conversations. Not only have our topics shifted because we heard each other, but our process has become ever more respectful of, and receptive to, differing views. Together, we are striving to make a better world for this generation and those that will follow us. I firmly believe that differences need not divide our efforts for peace and wellbeing.

Dialogue takes time, and I want to thank you, the reader, for taking the time to enter into this conversation. I write this from Ireland, where north and south are now competing with each other only for economic advantage. There's still the heavy sadness that it took so many years, lives, and loss before peace and reconciliation replaced war and fatigue. Can we not replace war with dialogue? Will our generation be the one to say "enough"?

Connemara, County Galway, Ireland
January 2008

CHAPTER ONE

An Unlikely Voice

I would be the first to admit that I am an unusual person to be offering my thoughts on Islam. I grew up in northern Indiana and lived on a farm that produced acres of corn as far as the eye could see. I went to Catholic boarding school at age thirteen, and then, at age seventeen, after high school graduation in 1961, I entered Our Lady of Grace monastery in Indiana.[1] In 1994, I assumed the role of Executive Director for Monastic Interreligious Dialogue (MID). This group, consisting mostly of monastics, sponsors formal inter-religious dialogues—mainly with Asian religions that have a monastic component.[2] I was two years into my role as Executive Director when I first met Islam. For seven years, I have participated in a series of formal Muslim–Catholic dialogues sponsored by the United States Conference of Catholic Bishops. Each year we have met in Indianapolis or the adjacent town of Plain-field, where we have been hosted by Dr. Sayyid M. Syeed of the Islamic Society of North America.

In spite of my personal commitment to dialogue, and even though we have had several thousand guests each year who have visited us at our retreat and conference center, Benedict Inn, and have hundreds of guests at the monastery itself, I do not recall that we have ever welcomed any Muslims for dinner in our refectory. We must prepare for this hospitality. This book, therefore, is my food for thought, my gift of welcome for my Muslim brothers and sisters. It is also my offer of introduction to Islam for the brothers and sisters of my own faith, and for all Christians who seek to understand Islam and its billion devotees throughout the world.

This book is written from the perspective of someone who has spent every day of the seven years of Muslim–Catholic dialogue in dialogue with and practicing her own faith. As a Benedictine nun, I have studied the origin of our monastic order in the sixth century and see the value of grasping the spiritual life as envisioned by the founder of our order, St. Benedict (c.480–c.547). I am grateful for the opportunity to look at Islam as I would look at Benedict's teaching. What is the way of life that both were imparting? What do St. Benedict and Muhammad embody for their followers?

For Christians, Jesus Christ is the Son of God, and the Qur'an holds him up as a great prophet— Muslims believe that Jesus was born miraculously and that he performed many miracles. While there are, clearly, substantial doctrinal differences between Christianity and Islam, there are, nonetheless, parallels. Muslims have the same relationship to the Qur'an as the word of God as Christians do to Christ, the Word of God. On a more personal level, because I follow the Rule of St. Benedict, I know how it feels to revere a human founder and to follow that human founder's path. Even though we know little about the historical Benedict, we nevertheless have a Rule that was written by him and clearly teaches the monastic way of life. Both Muslims and Benedictines, therefore, recognize that historical biography cannot explain fully the call to follow a practice.

This is why it is my belief that to understand Islam we must, as it were, "get underneath" the genius of Muhammad and see how Islam embodies the message he received from God as it has manifested itself in the lives of my Muslim friends attempting to live that message. Historical fact and biography aside, all I truly "know" about Islam from my own experience is what I see embodied in the Muslims at the table of dialogue. The challenge for me is to live my Christian way of life in such a manner that my Muslim friends "catch" the spirit of Christ just as I believe I have "caught" their Muslim way of life. It is thus in this spirit that I set out my understanding of Islam—I have received the beauty of this noble path and hope to convey that beauty to you.

While I am sure that I will never comprehend Islam as a member of that family of faith would, I feel that my warm experience, such as it is, has allowed me to "meet" the faith with honesty and humility. In the pages that follow I intend to share my "meeting" with the profoundly complex and sacred tradition of Islam. We who call ourselves Christians are at a turning point in our relationship with Muslims in our shared world. The wars in Afghanistan and Iraq, and the effort of the international community to combat terrorism, all require us to look deeply into the heart of Islam and its faith, its plurality of cultures and civilization. If we do not, we miss a jewel in our midst and risk generations upon generations of conflict because of ignorance.

Not only do I write as someone who is a practitioner and has been involved in interreligious dialogue with Buddhists and Hindus, I also write as a woman. As a woman, I have come to understand that women religious face unique challenges within their respective traditions. Catholic women religious face some common issues with Muslim women—from obtaining recognition as religious leaders to having the right even to speak and be respected as equals. My approach, however, has been neither to confront nor to walk away. It has been helpful for me to ask questions and, more importantly, to listen and try to make sense of what I see rather than simply stand back and observe. I have also sought to reclaim women's roles wherever it is possible. In this, I am not an advocate so much as a woman who simply practices her faith to the fullest extent of my capabilities. When I was the superior of my monastic community I performed my role alongside the ordained chaplain. In some ways, it would be taking the easy option to sit back and complain that I cannot preside at Eucharist, and choose to refuse to preside over the rituals that a non-ordained woman may conduct without further permission from a bishop. Instead of focusing on what I cannot do, however, I have done what I can.

In the dialogue with my Muslim friends, I do the same thing. In this way, I am at the table and engaged, and I have experienced being heard by my male dialogue partners at the meetings. However, this has been a challenge. In the first two years of the Muslim–Catholic dialogue I was the only woman. Now there are other women more competent than I, such as Sister Joan McGuire from the archdiocese of Chicago, who are engaged in the dialogue, and this delights me. We are in this dialogue together.

The biggest misconception that has greeted me in the seven years of Muslim–Catholic dialogue has been the thought that my belief in Jesus the Son of God and the Trinity would be a barrier to our further under-standing of one another, since Muslims see the Qur'an

and not Jesus as the Word of God. However, I have
been pleased and awestruck at my Muslim dialogue
partners' connection with and consciousness of God—
the same God I love and obey—whom I call God the
Father and whom they call God with no Second.
Therefore, while Muslims differ from Catholics,
without a doubt we can affirm one another in our way
of life under this same God that transcends all of us.

I have discovered that when you are in dialogue, an
amazing phenomenon occurs: You share your faith and
listen respectfully as the Buddhist, Hindu, Taoist, or
Muslim shares his or her heart's desire. What happens
is that you begin to "feel" that what they are experi-
encing is the same as what you feel in your own heart.
There is no need to correct one another's view; instead,
there is a real and mutual acceptance of each other's
way. You acknowledge to yourself that while their way
may not be your way, you are bearing witness to the
integrity of their way and it feels sound, good, and true.
This may seem counterintuitive—after all, so many of
our religious traditions have doctrinal distinctions that
sometimes appear to make dialogue impossible. Nevertheless, it is my experience that one's differences need
not divide. Our differences are real, and those differences are not merely nothing to worry about; instead,
they are worth celebrating, because they are the truth!

In the flash of time that these years of dialogue
represent, my faith has grown deeper because of

dialogue. I have found real friendship—a friendship not of submerged identities but one where our unique and distinct religions emerge. We can even promote the "other" religion while being wholly faithful to our own. The Buddhist scholar Joseph Goldstein talks about "not knowing" as a respectful way of letting two views live side by side. I feel that the practice of dialogue is one of "not knowing." That said, from the inside it feels like I "know" how that religion feels for me. It seems that in deepest dialogue in friendship with each other we share the same dimension of the one, true, and universal experience of the holy. Indeed, whenever we become overly "literal" in the interpretation of our faith and insist on a linear logic to express it, the mystery that holds so much of our religious practice and feelings is diminished.

During these years, I have entered through the doors of the world's sacred scriptures with awe and trembling. I have sought as much as possible to put aside preconceptions and prejudices, and opened my heart to receive those scriptures reverently and apprehend what grace makes present for me. As I have said, I have no illusion that I will come to a full understanding or see into that scripture's revelations. Instead, I bow as deeply as I can and then return to my own Christian scriptures for the revelation of God that resonates with my baptismal initiation and monastic vows.

My dialogue partner in this book is Shahid Athar,
MD, whom I have asked to comment on this text in
two afterwords. I welcome his wisdom, wit, and
passion for truth, and hope that one day he will write
his own "take" on Catholics. In my years of East–West
dialogue, I have always taken the position of letting the
"other" define him- or herself and not feel the need to
speak for him or her. It is out of respect for this that I
have listened these last seven years to my Muslim
friends. Indeed, this little book was prompted by an
event of dialogue, a routine Monday noon luncheon
meeting with Serra Club International (an organization
set up to help those preparing for priesthood and the
vocational life) at the Southside (Indianapolis) Knights
of Columbus Hall. I asked three Muslim friends to
speak, and each respectfully declined as they had work
obligations. So I spoke on Islam myself, and the
response was overwhelming. My Catholic friends were
amazed and inspired; they had questions beyond my
capacity to answer. Because the dialogue continues, I
see the need for little books such as this one.

There are 1.2 billion Muslims, one billion
Catholics, and 500 million other Christians who share
our planet. It seems to me that the two dominant religions should have a "feel" for one another—since religion is in service for all of us humans on Earth. If this
book gives you something of that "feel," then it might
lead to a relaxation of tensions and a move toward
peace.

CHAPTER TWO

An Earthly Religion

⁓

During my graduate days at the Catholic University of America, I was taught the social sciences alongside my theological studies. This approach presents religion as a human craft, and teaches that God's revelation comes through the human voice in the context of the human condition. It shows us that religions have the brilliance of human institutions and the foibles of human mistakes and proclivities. There are many religions: Hinduism, Jainism, Sikhism, Confucianism, Zoroastrianism, Judaism, Christianity, Buddhism, Islam, to name the major rivers that have carried millions of peoples over time to their destinations. Yet it has been my experience that most members of a religion do not like to be completely bracketed in a particular religion, because that religion never names the full experience of being a devotee, an adherent, a disciple, a practitioner, or a believer. Religion, in short, is a name from the outside.

As students of religion, we made a distinction
between religion on the one side and Christianity on
the other. "Religion" was the word we used for the
cultural phenomenon, and—for us—Christianity was
the "way of Christ." Catholicism is a particular form
of the way to follow Christ. Even though this distinction offers an overly simple view of the world, I have
nevertheless found it helpful to separate the human
shortfalls from the sublime revelation.

In 1995, several of us involved in Monastic Interreligious Dialogue made a journey to northern India
and Tibet. His Holiness the Dalai Lama invited us to
take part in a formal dialogue with members of the
five lineages of Tibetan Buddhism. Eager to learn
about their religion and the distinctions between their
schools, we asked some of the Tibetans how their
particular form of Buddhism differed from Zen
Buddhism, as practiced in Japan, and Theravada
Buddhism, as practiced in Southeast Asia. Our question, however, turned out to be a non-question: we
knew more "about" Buddhism than these practitioners did. They had no feel for what we might call
the *landscape* of Buddhist practice; since they knew
their own practice from the inside, they felt there was
no need to survey the field of Buddhism as if they were
observers. It was a humbling moment of recognition
for all of us who seek to understand other religions.
Those of us who study religions as well as those who

are involved in interreligious dialogue soon find out that all talk is "outside" the experience.

A similar point was made to me by Dr. Thubten Norbu, the Dalai Lama's oldest brother. He told me that there was no such thing as Buddhism, only decent human beings. He was reminding me not to get caught up in the doctrinal distinctions and formalism of religion. That said, I feel that it helps to know the "family origins" of each religious practitioner, since I believe that such knowledge helps us to create and live in a society where pluralism flourishes. However, it is always people, not the religion, that matter.

* * *

Islam is a religion and a follower of Islam is a Muslim. A Muslim believes in the revelation of God through the Qur'an that was given to the most holy prophet, Muhammad (570–632). In Christianity, the revelation was the incarnation of Jesus Christ, and the followers then wrote the story of Jesus' words and deeds in an inspired text. For a Muslim, the Qur'an is God's word. This word was memorized and recited by professional memorizers during the lifetime of Muhammad. It was written down in the present order on leaves and parchment in classical Arabic. In my opinion, the key to understanding Islam is to "know" this prophet and respect the Qur'an as Islam's authentic revelation. It is important to take seriously what are known as the five pillars of Islam and to comprehend how effective they are in forming a people of God. Lastly, it is necessary to weave together a few main threads that bind the Muslim faith into an intelligible whole. These themes, which I will explore later on in this book, are as follows:

- The cultural context of the desert and Islam as a civilization
- The cohesiveness of the word/observance/ unmediated symbol system
- The beliefs in God's blessings through economic prosperity
- The notion of ascendancy that comes about through the belief that previous revelations in Judaism or Christianity have been fulfilled in Islam

It is important to understand what Islam is not. Islam does not have a monastic tradition. We monks and nuns live in an alternative culture that ritualizes all our work and prayer. Islam uses the world as its full stage and theater. There is no separation between the visible and invisible, the physical and the spiritual dimensions.

There are orders of people called Sufis. The origin of their name has been variously ascribed to the woolen (*suf*) cloths that they originally wore to set them apart; or from *ashab al-suffa*, the name for devout Muslims who used to sit in the first row of worshipers behind the Prophet; or from the Arabic word for "purity" (*safa*). Sufis practice a kind of Islamic mysticism in which they cultivate a direct and personal experience of God. Nevertheless, Sufis have never separated themselves out from ordinary family life and the marketplace, though they have an alternative "family," as in our Benedictine cenobitic or monastic tradition. According to my Hindu teacher, with whom I studied for five years, Sufis in India could be Hindu rather than Muslim and their expression of faith pre-dated Islam in origin. Later, their guru was a sheikh of Islam. Orders of Sufis with a lineage of enlightened sheikhs flourished throughout the Muslim world from the eighth and ninth centuries to the present day.

Islam also has no priesthood. It has no unifying leader like the Pope—although the question of leadership within Islam has been an issue of contentious division between the two major branches of Islam, Sunni and Shia. There is also no universal or authoritative way to speak for the tradition. There is no single doctrinal council of teachers, nor is there a system of provinces and dioceses, parishes and congregations, such as you find in the vast world of Christianity. Islam is an earthly religion that functions

more like a civilization with many diverse cultures
that keeps its face directly turned to the One God.
There is no Church to mediate it. The sacraments—if
one looks for a parallel system with Christianity—
consist of the Qur'an and ordinary life's blessings of
family and prosperity. There is no ritual table of
Eucharist where the word (the bread) is broken and
community is gathered. For Muslims, community is
actual and not symbolic. Christians recall Christ's
death on the cross ritually at Eucharist, symbolically
through gesture and in eating bread and drinking
wine, remembering Christ at the Altar of Sacrifice.
Professor Ewert Cousins suggests that when Shiite
men beat their chests in grief at the martyrdom of
Imam Hussein, grandson of the Prophet Muhammad,
in the solemn festival of Muharram, it reflects a
similar and ancient impulse to sacrifice oneself as
one's leader was in turn sacrificed.

I will begin by looking at the life of Muhammad.

Who Was Muhammad?

Muslims do not believe that the Holy Prophet
Muhammad was an incarnation of God, nor do they,
like Christians, believe that Jesus was the Son of God
and an indivisible part of God. Muslims believe that
Muhammad was a man and that he followed Adam,
Abraham, Moses, David, Solomon, and Jesus as the
last of the great prophets to receive divine revelation.

Muhammad was born in Mecca (in what is now Saudi Arabia) in 570, and his early childhood was marked by loss. Muhammad's father Abdullah died before he was born, and his paternal grandfather, Abdul Muttalib, assumed responsibility for his upbringing. Then his mother Aminah died when he was six, and his grandfather died two years later. When Muhammad grew up, he became a merchant, traveling as far as Yemen and Syria with his uncle, Abu Talib. On these long journeys, Muhammad mixed with Christians and Jews, and was attracted to the notion of the One God. He felt keenly that the Arabians, who worshiped many gods at that time, were bereft of a calling to the One God.

Muhammad was also acutely aware of the unjust distribution of wealth and the plight of the poor—the masses of people who had no access to the necessities of food, clothing, and shelter in the harsh climate of the desert where everything was scarce. Mecca was a major trading center, with goods moving between Yemen and the Mediterranean regions of Gaza and Damascus. While the town was prosperous, Muhammad saw how the money was concentrated in only a few hands and how tribal divisions and individual greed not only threatened the stability of the clans and tribes but also impeded the traditional Arab custom of helping the poor.

When Muhammad was forty years old and under-

going his period of solitude in the mountains (as was a
practice of the devout in his time) he experienced a
profoundly life-changing mystical experience. Through
the mediation of the angel Gabriel, Muhammad
received the first in a series of revelations, which came
to him over a period of twenty years. He shared these
with his cousin Ali and his beloved wife Khadijah,
whom he had married when he was twenty-four years
old and who was sixteen years his senior. They encouraged him to speak more widely of what he saw and to
recite the inspired vision to others.

Muhammad was a respected merchant but could
neither read nor write. This point is critical in understanding his shock at this transcendent event.
Muhammad tested the authenticity of his revelations
with prayer and fasting, and it was two years before
he went public with his profound religious experience. Those who heard him were caught up in his
enthusiasm and the truthfulness of the transmission,
which came in full, poetic, graceful Arabic that was
beyond his personal capacity to compose or contrive.
(Christians will recall Christ's disciples at Pentecost,
when the rural fishermen were touched by flame and
began speaking in tongues and with an eloquence
that astonished the crowd who listened.)
Muhammad spoke with conviction of Allah, the One
God, and told his listeners that he had profoundly
surrendered to Allah. From this came Muhammad's

powerful understanding that, after one experiences God, it is impossible to do anything than simply and totally "surrender"—the literal meaning of the word *islam*.

Muhammad was awestruck by his revelations. He thought and felt like a prophet, such as those in the Hebrew scriptures and like Jesus in the Christian story, except he felt no claim to be Son of God, only a messenger. From what he knew from his travels of the lineage of the Jews and Christians, they were like him descendants of Abraham. Over time, he understood his vocation to welcome the Arabian peoples to return to Abraham's God. However, he met with a number of reverses. He was surprised to find out that the Jews did not accept another prophet for another people. Furthermore, there was opposition to the recitations, as the verses Muhammad spoke were called, from the rich merchant class in Mecca. They felt threatened by his criticism of their lives and his increasing influence among the Arabs, whom he was beginning to gather to follow his leadership. The merchants began to undermine Muhammad.

After the death of Khadijah and his uncle in 619, Muhammad lost the support of another uncle, Abu Lahab, who withdrew protection from him and left him exposed to personal attacks. Muhammad then left Mecca, ending up in the nearby town of Medina. Muhammad's flight from Mecca is called the *hijrah* or "emigration." It is from this moment that the official Muslim calendar begins.

The move to Medina initiated a new phase in Muhammad's life. In Medina, Muhammad began to set in motion the ways of life that would lead to the surrender to God. These were: the worship of Allah five times a day, sharing wealth with the poor, reciting the Qur'an, fasting, and proclaiming the central doctrine of Islamic faith: "There is no God but God, and Muhammad is His messenger." These are called the five pillars of Islam. This orderly way of life, under a unifying God (Allah), was particularly attractive to the Bedouin tribes who lived around the region, and it was soon taken up by more and more desert dwellers and merchants in exchange for the safety that they got by gathering as a cohesive unit. Like many other groups in the region at the time, Muhammad's followers engaged in raids (*razzias*) on caravans as a way of redistributing wealth. As harsh though these raids seem to us now, they were an expected hazard for those who lived in and made their passage through the desert. Indeed, the defense against attack and attacking vans themselves seem to have been part of the ordinary rhythm of life at the time.

At first, Muhammad was gentle in his approach and nonviolent even with his enemies, especially those based in Mecca who by now felt very threatened by the power base that Muhammad had built for himself in Medina. After some years of loss and victory in battle on both sides, the turning point in Muhammad's fortunes occurred in 627, where the Meccans laid siege to Muhammad's followers near Medina. Even though the Meccans had promised to destroy Muhammad, they failed to dislodge his forces. This success fueled Muhammad's confidence and was seen by him and others as a sign of Allah's favor. Muhammad continued to preach Islam to Meccans with fervor. At last, he entered Mecca in triumph in 630.

The shift of consciousness that occurred with Muhammad's success and earthly prosperity and the solidarity felt by the followers of the new religion allowed the development of a community of believers, called an *umma*. Under God, these tribes and clans transcended their territorial and family boundaries, and consolidated their possessions, family ties, and identifying characteristics. In this way, Muslims envisioned the religion of Islam. God was the center, Muhammad was the leader, and the Qur'an was the Word of God from which all Muslims could find sustenance.

In the last years of Muhammad's life and shortly after his death in 632, Islam spread with lightning speed throughout the Middle East—borne on the wings of Muhammad's consolidation of Arabian tribes under Islam and his rapid rise to preeminence in

the region. After the Persian Empire defeated the
Byzantine Empire in 628, minority tribes in Yemen
and other parts of Arabia, who had been under
Byzantine security, turned to Muhammad for protection and converted to Islam. In 630, Muhammad took
his followers on a campaign that reached the borders
of Syria, an event that brought him into conflict with
Christians. Between 634 and 650 Muslim forces
routed Byzantine and Persian armies, and took
control of Libya, Egypt, Palestine, Syria, Iraq, and
most of modern-day Iran (Persia).[1] By the end of the
eighth century, Islam had reached central Asia and
India, and had spread across Mediterranean Africa
and into Spain and France, where its spread was
halted at the Battle of Poitiers in 732.

Muhammad's death was sudden, and there was no
obvious successor to take his place as temporal and
spiritual leader of the Arabs. The resulting instability
led to many years of struggle and dissension among
his followers—particularly between those who
followed Muhammad's son-in-law Ali (known as
Shiites) and those who wished another follower, Abu
Bakr, to be leader. (Abu Bakr lived for only two years
after Muhammad's death and was followed as
caliph—which literally means "deputy of the
prophet"—by Umar and Uthman. It was this branch
of Islam that became known as Sunni.) Such dissension became common as the Arabs extended their

empire over an increasingly large geographic area, encompassing many different ethnic groups and cultural practices. Indeed, the rise of Shia Islam in the 640s was a response to the increasing worldliness of Sunni Islam as it took over the Persian Empire and made inroads into the Byzantine Empire. It is worth noting at this point that Caliph Umar pledged protection of the Jews when his forces took Jerusalem in 641, and that it was the Christian Bishop of Egypt who invited the Muslims to enter his country to displace the Romans.

The Character of Muhammad

So, who was Muhammad? According to the early twentieth-century English biographer, Stanley Lane-Poole, Muhammad

> was of the middle height, rather thin, but broad of shoulders, wide of chest, strong of bone and muscle. His head was massive, strongly developed. Dark hair, slightly curled, flowed in a dense mass down almost to his shoulders. Even in advanced age it was sprinkled by only about twenty grey hairs. . . . His face was oval-shaped. . . . Fine, long, arched eyebrows were divided by a vein which throbbed visibly in moments of passion. Great black restless eyes shone out from under long,

heavy eyelashes. His nose was large, slightly
aquiline. His teeth upon which he bestowed
great care were well set, dazzling white. . . . A
full beard framed his manly face. His skin was
clear and soft, his complexion "red and
white," his hands were as "silk and satin.". . .
His step was quick and elastic, yet firm, and as
that of one "who steps from a high to a low
place." In turning his face he would also turn
his full body. His whole gait and presence were
dignified and imposing. His countenance was
mild and pensive. His laugh was rarely more
than a smile.[2]

Beyond this physical description, we know that
Muhammad was a saintly man. He had seven children: three sons who died at birth and four daughters
who also died young. Only Muhammad's daughter
Fatima was living at the time of his death. He was
devoted to his first wife Khadijah until her death,
although he later had other wives, as was the custom
at the time. Reports show him to be very charismatic,
fast-speaking, but prone to silence. He was vigorous
and yet gentle, especially with children. Although he
had much success on the battlefield, he lived more like
an ascetic than a general or imperial ruler. He coun-
seled measured action in response to adversity.
Although by nature solitary, he nonetheless was very

involved in the life of the community and his family, apart from the month of Ramadan. More than anything else, however, he seemed totally engaged in his relationship with God.[3]

Muhammad was a prophet, a visionary, a family man who had children, and a political and religious leader who pulled together many clans and followers to surrender before the One God, Allah. He transmitted a sense of awe to a family of believers under the One God who would protect, guide, and bring them to the promised life in the next world but also bless them abundantly in this earthly life. A Muslim would say that Muhammad's greatest contribution to the world was to mediate the word of God that we know today as the Qur'an—the central scripture that proclaims that Allah is One for 1.2 billion Muslims around the world, and holds communities from Jakarta to Lahore and Indianapolis to Cape Town together.

CHAPTER THREE

The Pillars of Islam

⁀

1. The Profession of Faith

As indicated earlier, there are five pillars to Islam. The first pillar is the Muslims' ultimate profession of their faith, the *shahada*: *la ilaha illa Allah; Muhammad rasul Allah*, "There is no god but Allah, and Muhammad is the prophet of Allah." This confession is repeated at least five times each day by the *muezzin* in the minaret of every mosque around the world as an invitation to prayer. Just as it is impossible to exaggerate the importance of the Qur'an for a devout Muslim, so it would be hard to exaggerate how central this first pillar of belief is. The belief in the one, transcendent God is the pole around which the whole religion orbits. Muslims believe in a dualistic universe: there is an "other," and that "other" is the created person or thing, distinct from, but in relationship with, the One God. This dualistic dynamic sets up the proper response to the God who created the creature. God is transcendent and full of mystery and

41

in every dimension. There is no other like God, no modifier. God, simply, is God.

While Islam traditionally lists ninety-nine names that praise and glorify God, revealing some of God's characteristics (the subtle, the nourisher, the watcher, the originator, etc.), Christians need to understand that there is no possibility of division or distinction, as there is in the Christian notion of the Trinity, or in the idea of Christ, whom Christians consider to be both God and human. In Islam there are no exceptions to the indivisibility of the notion and facticity of God and His Oneness. Notice that there are two distinctions here that differ from the Christian notion of God: first, God is One, not Trinity, and secondly, this oneness conversely shows that any differentials would diminish God as God, so God's One-ness is what it means to be God. Nevertheless, in spite of these deep doctrinal differences with Christianity, all Muslims honor the monotheistic traditions of Christianity and Judaism because we worship the One God. We are all "people of the book," a testament to the respect that Islam has not only for scholarship but also for the wisdom contained in the Hebrew and Christian scriptures.

The transcendence of God is the dominant belief for a Muslim. No image, doctrine, or dogmas can postulate the reality. The recognition of this transcendence is sacred enough to cause the complete and total surrender of a creature. This was the main message of Muhammad, who saw himself as reminding all peoples of the reality of God's transcendence. Muhammad argued that the old patterns of the old gods could not protect anyone, only Allah could. The attractiveness of such a doctrine at that time and place was clear—spiritual malaise and constant and destructive internecine strife that violated all the tribal codes and traditions of Arabia made the clarity and compassion of the all-merciful God attractive. Henceforth, all Muslims were part of an increasingly global community, *umma*, which was governed by justice and equity (see Armstrong, *Islam*, p. 8). The surrender implicit in the *shahada* is not just assented to notionally but is actually observed by the Muslim through the other four pillars of Islam. The personal and individual human's surrender is the way of salvation. There is no mercy through a human savior; every person must bend his will and lift up his mind in assent to God's transcendence, and God will reward the adherent with mercy and a life hereafter. One is a Muslim to the extent one appropriates the God-consciousness of Allah. There is no baptism or membership without practice. The five pillars literally sustain the faith.

This practice is not unlike a Christian's way of ceaseless prayer (1 Thessalonians 5:17). The mantra of *shahada* echoes in the heart and mind. It is a form of concentration, focus, and total approbation. It does not concern itself with being *about* something. It is neither speculative nor philosophical in orientation. Instead, the *shahada* plunges through levels and levels of consciousness to penetrate the core of one's heart in a way of belief that is linked with prayer and pure moral conduct. With a clear mind one can make poised, thoughtful choices, provided with a constant awareness of God that is nourished with routine, daily and prescribed prayer.

2. Prayer

The second pillar of Islam is prayer (*salaat*), which is carried out five times a day: at dawn, noon, mid-afternoon, sunset, and after the fall of darkness or at bedtime. The actual prayers are accompanied by ritual cleansing, hand gestures, body bows and prostrations, and prescribed rubrics that apply whether you pray alone or with others.

I have personally seen this act of prayer many times. At the mosque in Plainfield, Indiana, women can watch the prayers and join from the back as the men line up and do the prayer with utmost devotion and precision. Each man and woman prepares for the prayer through a ritual of ablution. They stand reverently in a straight line, offering certain prayers, bowing toward Mecca with hands on knees. They do not so much as offer Allah petitions, as Christians might think of prayers, but rather ascriptions or praise and declarations of submission to His holy will. The devotees straighten up, still praising Allah, then fall prostrate, kneeling with head to the ground, glorifying God. They then sit up reverentially and offer a petition. Finally, they bow again. Throughout this practice, the sacred sentence *Allahu akbar* ("God is great") is repeated again and again. It is common at the beginning simply to repeat the *fatiha*, which consists of the first words of the first *sura* of the Qur'an. Christians might consider this to be the equivalent of the Lord's Prayer:

> Praise belongs to God, the Lord of all Being,
> The All-merciful, the All-compassionate,
> The Master of the Day of Doom.
> Thee only we serve, to Thee alone we pray for
>   succor.
> Guide us in the straight path,
> The path of those whom Thou hast blessed,
> Not of those against whom Thou are wrathful,
> Nor of those who are astray. (See Noss,
>   p. 607)

Sometimes, usually on Friday at noon, one of the men stands before the devotees and offers words of inspiration. It is essential for Muslims to make the ground of prayer holy. On one occasion, when our

Catholic–Muslim dialogue was taking place at Fatima
Retreat House in Indianapolis, my Muslim colleagues
insisted that the facility provide sheets to stand on so
that they could make the floor a holy ground. I know
individuals who travel with their own prayer rug to
roll out for their *salaat* wherever they are. Once, while
I was waiting at Chicago's O'Hare airport to catch a
flight, I walked into the chapel and was surprised to
see more Muslims than Christians saying midday
prayers. At another interreligious dialogue event in
Chicago, I visited a mosque and sat with the other
women behind an ornate screen as prayers were
conducted.

The fact that Muslims pray five times a day is dear
to my heart since, as a Benedictine nun, I too pray five
times a day. Our Divine Office is morning, noon, and
evening, with mass and night prayers. I have
witnessed and participated in the same prayer rhythm
at Buddhist and Hindu monasteries. Clearly, what is
common to all these religions is a human desire to
sanctify the hours in an orderly way. It is a way for us
to recognize that if there is a God then we must turn
to God and bow. In the Buddhist traditions, of course,
practitioners bow not to God but to Buddha-nature or
the deities that share the realm of Clear Light.

The practice of regular prayer throughout the day
gives to time nothing more nor less than *graciousness*.
The practice turns time inside out. What in my early

years of monastic life was an interruption to my day (all that stopping for prayers and starting again) turned into a ceaseless and seamless way of being in time. For Benedictines, prayer is itself embodied in work. We pray without ceasing. And there is, undoubtedly, strength in numbers—about being called to gather in a particular place to pray together. It is easier for our practice if, at the beginning, middle, and end of the day and sometimes in between, we join with other like-minded souls.

Morning, noon, and night offer a natural impulse of the human spirit to rise and give praise. When I was present for the Muslim *salaat*, I felt as though I was at home with my nuns in Beech Grove, Indiana. It was the same God, the same praise, and the same bended knee. This is why, as a gesture of solidarity with my Muslim friends, every morning after a twenty-minute sit in the oratory I bow my forehead to the floor. I am not sure I am pointing toward any city here on Earth, let alone Mecca, as I sometimes sit in a different seat in the oratory. However, I am sure it is the same God to whom Muslims and Catholics alike direct our hearts.

The other similarity that exists between the religions in this regular kind of daily short prayer is the humility such practice requires. When the call to prayer is made you have to stop what you are doing and go to chapel or the mosque. There is no fudging

or promising to pray twice as hard later. You have to
leave your computer, your hoe, or your basket. There
is a higher power that rightfully claims your time, over
and over again, commanding you to acknowledge
your submission and allowing you to respond "yes"
over and over again to that demand: "God is God and
I obey." This is a right relationship.

Although we Benedictines and Muslims practice
prayer as a form of worship, it is the practice in
humility that makes it more readily possible to cease
and desist doing our will when we should refrain and
act on behalf of the other. This makes our aspiration
an actual behavioral practice of moving from my self-
centeredness toward another. The daily prayer practice provides me with the energy to give my goods as
well as my time. Islam is an ingenious system of such
energy direction—creating a spiritual *economy* (literally "the law of the home") not so much in the life
hereafter (as in the salvation of Jesus Christ) but right
now on Earth. For me, the benefit of all the prescribed
prayer times is to secure the ceaseless prayer as a firm
practice. I don't get far from prayer in my mind and
heart; instead, I return to it over and over again.
When I go through dry periods, my mind might
wander during prayer; but my body is there and I do
the rituals with exact form. Eventually, my heart is
restored to warmth.

There is great power in the group. My community

of eighty-five nuns carries me when my devotion is tepid. I see that same zeal among my Muslim friends. The stopping for prayer is the norm, allowing us to be God-conscious during the in-between times and to help God-consciousness become pervasive. What then happens is that we return to ritual prayer thankful for this felt presence of God. The combination of frequent gathering for prayer (as we do in the Divine Office) and the ceaseless prayer we do in our personal prayer (like saying the Jesus Prayer) allows us to keep the memory of God ever present. Doing this shifts consciousness from remembering that God is present to an abiding experience of God's Presence.

Many in the Christian world find the idea of ceaseless prayer strange. One time a classmate from my days at college stopped by the monastery and we were catching up after years of separation. "What do you do all day?" she asked me. How could I get anything done with all that prayer? Wasn't I tired of being a nun after forty years? I had no answer for her. This was the way I lived and the way all of us at the monastery lived. There was nothing else. It is in this lived reality—and the all-encompassing nature of it— whereby I feel kinship with Islam. We serve others—a natural outcome of all the praying.

3. Almsgiving (*zakat*)

The third pillar of Islam involves a serious redistribution of wealth. Since all is given by God, then nothing of what I own is mine, unless it is shared according to God's will. Muslims traditionally give 2.5 percent of their wealth to the poor, although this tithing sometimes has taken the form of a tax if the government is Muslim. Nevertheless, the intent remains the same: to give to the poor and to be a just and peace-filled society.

The principle of almsgiving stems from Muhammad's alarm at the sight of the poor during his early days as a traveling merchant. He witnessed the unjust burden of the masses and the opulence of the ruling families, and decided that he and his followers would make sure that the poor had food, clothing, and shelter. He saw that all creatures belonged to God and that Allah would repay each according to their good deeds on Earth and in heaven.

Muhammad had a keen sense of the hereafter, and the Qur'an describes heaven and the final days of Earth with rich imagery. At one of our dialogues, my Muslim friends and I talked about how we viewed the afterlife. The Muslims had clear portraits of the afterlife. We explained that as Catholics we had only the belief in the afterlife and that, while there is a rich artistic heritage depicting the afterlife, for Catholics the Bible does not provide a portrait. The revelation in the Qur'an is that in this world the rich must give to the poor to guarantee a place in heaven with the angels and Allah. In practice, therefore, almsgiving is an insurance policy to be entitled to heaven. The gathering of alms also exemplifies to Muslims that they are an *umma*, a community.

Such generosity is based on two teachings. First, as we have seen, all goods are gifts of God and God has told us to share them. Secondly, these gifts are blessings and rewards from God, and will be taken away if not used rightly. For Muslims, giving to the poor is not optional; it is the duty of bowing with one's goods. There are no exceptions—all are expected to give annually. In practice, this means that a Muslim who makes $40,000 gives about $1,000 off the net income.

The pillar of almsgiving seems eminently sensible, not only because a just society requires equity but because of the basic belief that earthly prosperity is the sacrament whereby God is mediated from heaven to Earth. Jews and Muslims establish a "this-worldly" goal of economic wellbeing as the proof of God's blessings. Muslims also have these riches continuing in a heavenly realm. Muslims believe that God wants His peoples to prosper and to live in rich abundance. Therefore, grace is not invisible, but instead visible through family, offspring, property, security, and good order.

(As you can see, the pillars of Islam build an edifice. God is. God is One. There is no other God than Allah. Surrender. Obey, pray, and create a just

and peaceful society. Recite praise to Allah. Bow
heads and bend knees five times a day. Give what has
been given to those in need.)

In writing this, I know that there are Muslims, just
as there are Christians, who are devout practitioners,
and those who claim the name but dismiss the laws
and customs. I suspect this might be true of all religious traditions. My feelings are that, as a large religion, Islam has room for all degrees of involvement.
There is a strong belief in Islam that Allah will judge
you, and there are many pictures of reward and
punishment in the afterlife. Consequent to the idea of
almsgiving and to the sense of judgment for one's life,
Islam strongly hints at egalitarianism in daily life
before there is eternal life. Giving to the poor is not a
matter of mercy or charity on the devotee's behalf. It
is a matter of justice.

For the Muslim, God does not plan for his creatures to be poor. A Muslim feels blessed for being alive
and understands that he is created by God and so
surrenders his life to God. As part of his surrender
(*islam*) the Muslim provides for the poor and thus
receives God's mercy and goodness through economic
prosperity. This instills more gratitude as well as
salvation in the hereafter, which stimulates still further
surrender. In this way, Islam is firm, dynamic, and
actual—a universal pattern that God first set in
motion at the Creation.

It is more than "a shame" to have the poor in our midst. For a Muslim, to mingle with the poor offends sensibilities and the Muslim has a mandate to do something about it. In fact, Muslims' eternal salvation depends on their response to justice. Where Christianity historically has been concerned about right doctrine (orthodoxy), Islam was from its inception primarily a way of right living (orthopraxy). In fact, not only could one argue that Islam is a response to pagan Arabia's failure to deal with poverty, but it is also a "reformation" of sixth-century Christian and Jewish indifference to the inequalities between rich and poor.

In Islam, the leadership is predominantly lay— although the distinction between lay and clergy has its own particular character since Shiite imams may sometimes behave in the same way as clergy. Nevertheless, it is fair to say that there is no Church or priestly class between the Muslim and God. There are mosques that are centers of worship, as well as of learning and study of the Qur'an, and these may raise up an imam as a leader. However, there is no formal ordination ceremony. The imams I have met qualified for their position by reciting the Qur'an and living the life with exactitude. As a religion, Islam has the minimum amount of infrastructure that requires overhead and maintenance. A mosque (the word itself literally means "a place to prostrate") is often stun-

ningly beautiful architecturally and can be brilliantly
ornate. However, all semblance of opulence is to be
avoided and most staff workers are volunteers. The
money collected usually goes to those in need through
education loans, financial opportunities, or in the
basics of food, medicine, clothing, and shelter in the
attendees' countries of origin, many of which have
been devastated by war.

Mosques have regular training for children, and
provide places for marriage and funerals as well as
the ongoing socialization of the Muslim way of life.
In Plainfield, Indiana, the mosque has a full-time staff
member who helps to arrange marriages and assists
the next generation in perpetuating their Muslim
heritage.

It has been a gradual revelation to me how closely
interwoven in community and family are the lives of
my Muslim friends. Catholicism in America has been
through the turn of modernity and the secularism and
separation of Church and State. First-generation
Muslims have come to the United States from a
variety of countries that have kept the sacredness of
their faith with a worldview where there has been no
separation of the religion of Islam from being a
Muslim, an American, a doctor, a father, a husband,
etc. In this regard, their lives mirror my own as a nun.
When asked what our mission is, nuns respond that
our monastic way of life is God's way for us and is a

benefit for all humankind. I believe a Muslim would say that Islam is the whole of his or her way of life, with nothing outside of it. It deserves, and gets, total loyalty and commitment.

4. Ramadan

The fourth pillar of Islam is the fast that takes place during the holy month of Ramadan, the ninth month of the Muslim calendar. It lasts from the first sighting of the crescent moon until the next first sighting of the crescent moon, which ends the fasting with a meal of celebration. The emblem of the crescent moon is an identifying symbol for Islam. All Muslims all over the world during Ramadan are called on to fast for thirty days, unless they are sick or on a journey. The aim of abstaining from food during the day is to help Muslims identify with the poor, who cannot choose when, where, and what to eat. In this way, fasting is similar in intention to almsgiving. Because the Muslim calendar has 354 or 355 days in it, Ramadan each year occurs ten days earlier than the previous year, although the length of time the fasting occurs is always thirty days. As David Noss puts it:

[A]s soon as it becomes possible at dawn to distinguish a white thread from a black one, no food or drink may be taken until sun-down; then enough food or drink should be

consumed to enable one to fast the next day
without physical weakness (Noss, p. 546).

Several traditions have grown up regarding the meal
that occurs after the sun has gone down. For some, the
meal is a time of celebration and storytelling. For
others it is an ascetical practice of remembering the
Prophet, his mission, and all the hardships he endured
in the name of God. The close of the month is usually
celebrated in a great festival called *Eid*. Just as Easter
is a time of joy at the end of Lent, so Eid is a time when
the purification that fasting provides can be truly felt.

Fasting is a practice that appears in some manner
through all the major religions, and it has major benefits. Voluntary fasting sets one apart from the
mundane, gives them discipline, and provides a physical dimension to beliefs that otherwise might simply
be only an assent of words. Fasting necessitates
resisting one's needs and desires and self-will by
surrendering them to God's will.

In comparison with some practices of fasting in
other world religions, Ramadan is a moderate fast. It
only lasts one month and takes place only during the
daylight hours. It requires no special foods and can be
done by anyone anywhere. Like other fasts, it teaches
discernment and creates a culture of restraint. The fast
from food and drink takes place in the midst of the
ordinary day, during which each Muslim prays five

times a day and does his duty of work. During Ramadan, the Muslim is to refrain from sexual activity—a practice that, along with the training of thirty days of fasting with a like-minded group, exemplifies and influences other forms of restraint from self-indulgence. As suggested before, there is a direct link between fasting and almsgiving. The observant Muslim is called to surrender, again not in idealism, but in actuality and at an ordinary level whereby fasting is simply seen as what it means to be a Muslim. In other words, these practices are not, as Christians might imagine, the higher practices of a saint. They are the expected minimum activity of ordinary people.

5. Pilgrimage

The fifth pillar of Islam also bonds a community of believers. It is the pilgrimage (*hajj*) to Mecca. This obligation does what all great pilgrimages do: it restarts the conversion experience by returning the devotee to the point of origin. A religion is not just a collectivity, but consists of many clusters of individuals who must take on themselves again the beliefs and practices of the founder of the religion and the dictates of the religion's scriptures. To take a sacred journey, along with other believers, is to personally accept and immerse oneself in the culture of that religion and make it your own.

The customs surrounding the Muslim pilgrimage
are instructive. All men, and all women accompanied
by a male, can do the *hajj* if they can afford it. In the
ceremony, all males, whether rich or poor, enter the
precincts of Mecca wearing the same kind of seamless
white garments. They practice the proper absti-
nence—no food or drink by day, sexual continence,
and no harm to living things. No exceptions are made
for class, race, or nationality. The ritual takes the form
of a circumambulation of the *Kaaba*, a sacred stone of
great religious significance in pagan Arabia that main-
tained its sacredness in Islam. Legend has it that God
gave the stone to Adam on his expulsion from para-
dise so that his sins could be forgiven.

The pilgrims start at the Kaaba and run three times
fast and four times slowly around the building that
houses the stone, stopping each time at the southeast
corner to kiss the stone itself. If the crowd is too great,
pilgrims can touch it with hand or stick or perhaps just
look at it with eagerness and devotion. It is said that
the stone used to be white in color, but turned black
from absorbing the sins of all the devotees who have
touched or kissed it. The next observance is the Lesser
Pilgrimage, which consists of trotting, with shoulders
shaking, seven times between Safa and Marwa, two
low hills across the valley from each other. This ritual
is in imitation of the frantic Hagar, the wife of
Abraham, desperately seeking water for her baby,

Ishmael, whose children are thought to be the ancestors of Muslims, just as Isaac, son of Abraham's wife
Sarah, is said to be patriarch of the Jews.

On the eighth day of the *hajj*, the Greater
Pilgrimage begins. The pilgrims, in a dense mass,
move off toward the Arafat plain, nine miles to the
east. They pass the night at Mina, a place halfway
between Mecca and Arafat. The next day, all pilgrims
arrive at the Arafat plain, where they engage in a
prayer service conducted by an imam, listen to his
sermon, and, of utmost importance, stand or move
slowly about, absorbed in pious meditation. After
sunset, they begin running en masse with enormous
joy and commotion to Muzdalifah, which is a
quarter of the distance back to Mecca, where they
pass the night in the open. At sunrise, they continue
to Mina, where each pilgrim casts seven pebbles at
three places (in order to ward off demons) down the
slope below the mountain road, crying out at each
throw, "In the name of God! Allah is almighty!"
Next there is a sacrificial offering of meat (to represent Abraham's sacrifice of the ram to God) and the
meat is eaten by all.

The three days following are spent in eating,
talking, and merrymaking, in the strictest continence,
and then as a final act of the pilgrimage all return to
Mecca and make the circuit of the Kaaba once more
(Noss, pp. 547–48).

Lest a non-Muslim reader mistake the *hajj* as a solely ethnic practice and bracket the pilgrimage with the great pilgrimages to Jerusalem, Arunachala in India, Mount Kailas in Tibet, or Lourdes in France, the Meccan pilgrimage is in a class of its own. There are over one billion Muslims in the world, and each male and female is required to make this pilgrimage once in his or her life. Young people are also admitted, which means that every year the numbers attending the *hajj* are huge—up to three million or more people at a time. Pilgrims must obtain a special visa stating that they are fit and observant Muslims. This pilgrimage of antiquity combines all the human and divine muscle to evoke and sustain conversion—travel from all nations of the world, the requirements of ritual purity, the wearing of special clothes, the walking over twenty miles, the night-sleep in open air, and the accommodations in tents pitched in the desert. It is an extraordinary effort of logistics and faith.

The recitation of the Qur'an in Arabic, the en masse salute, the fellowship of meals and hours of sharing and being a "people" surrendered to Allah make evident the literal meaning of religion as a "binding" to God. The *hajj* binds each Muslim to Allah and to every other Muslim. Uniquely, this binding is not restricted to the ordained or the vowed elite, or those who privilege a particular location for their form of devotion. To be a Muslim is to be beyond ethnic identity, and the pillar of this pilgrimage tells the story and incorporates each member, each generation, and the people as a whole into the revelation given to the Prophet. The total experience is one of surrender, while the feeling generated in each person is of being a descendent of Abraham under God.

In Christianity, we often use the image of the desert to describe an experience on our spiritual journey. Christianity's earliest monastic tradition in the third century began in a desert that within four centuries was—as it is now—mostly in Muslim countries. The monks and nuns of those early Christian settlements were not in community as we live it today. They were hermits who went out to live the solitary life, motivated by the goal of praying without ceasing and seeking God with their whole attention. They met their inner demons that were the afflictions of food, sex, material possessions, anger, depression, acedia (spiritual soul fatigue), vainglory, and pride. Grace prevailed.

These Desert Fathers and Mothers are the source of wisdom for the founder of the monastic order I live today as a Benedictine.

It is my belief that the desert of the pilgrimage expected of every Muslim is not unlike the protracted solitude in the desert, where the monastic faces his or her inner demons and surrenders his or her ego to

God in utmost humility. Christ, too, before the advent
of his ministry is driven by the Spirit into the desert to
be tested (Mark 1:12). The desert clarifies the mind
and purges the soul; it is real and symbolic. In the real
geographic location one must stay focused to survive;
one must get along with others to secure and maintain
goods; one must move quickly, lightly, and frequently
to have enough basics for food, shelter, clothing, and
human interaction. One must be tough enough to
travel long distances and defer one's needs to provide
for those who are weak. One must enjoy the solitude
and adapt to the harshness of the climate.

The landscape of the symbolic desert forces one to
cultivate an inner life, because there is no way to
avoid feeling again and again all the thoughts, desires,
and passions that rise when the external world offers
no distraction. The spiritual journey courses through
the soul without the noise of crowds or the pressures
of overwork. In such a situation a rawness or naked-
ness, a sense of being alone with the Alone, occurs.
Hermits push themselves to the edge of being bound
to the Earth in order to step out of time and into the
temple of God's presence. Given the power of the
desert, it makes sense that Muslims celebrate their
origins in Arabia and take a pilgrimage through the
desert in order to return to the core of their faith.

The *hajj* thus actualizes the inner life of the spiritual journey in a communal experience. Most of us

choose not to become hermits. However, it is reasonable to believe that once in our life we could make pilgrimage to Jerusalem or Mecca and in this way externalize our inner journey. By making the pilgrimage to Mecca one of its five pillars, Islam pulls together the meaning of the desert and the inner conversion necessary to surrender to one's depths during one's life. Once again, as we saw with fasting, it makes a serious religious practice—the inner spiritual journey—not simply a matter for saints or mystics or hermits. Islam makes the *hajj* a defining feature of being a Muslim.

In 1996, Monastic Interreligious Dialogue conducted a conference at Gethsemani Abbey, Kentucky (the home of Thomas Merton), where Buddhist and Christian monastics discussed their traditions in a spirit of tolerance and understanding. One of the attendees was His Holiness the Dalai Lama, who suggested that pilgrimage would be a fitting follow-up to the hospitality and the dwelling together with one heart we had experienced. The hardships of pilgrimage, he noted, in themselves provide the purifications necessary to remove obstacles to a clear mind and an open heart. The Dalai Lama said that pilgrimages situate dialogue on the human plane where there are no academic or doctrinal differences and no speculative talk about what someone else is doing somewhere else at another time. Pilgrimage is a human way that all humankind can be united in microcosm.

At the invitation of His Holiness the Dalai Lama we have been to Tibet and circumambulated the sacred sites with the Tibetan nomads. While the numbers were fewer than in Mecca, the zeal and absolute concentration in contemplative prayer shown by the pilgrims were life-changing and gave me something of an idea of what it must be like to be in Mecca. In the middle of these Buddhist nomads, at an altitude of 14,000 feet, I was swept into silence by the mantras, prayer wheels, and chants anointing my soul. I can only imagine that a pilgrimage in the desert to Mecca would be the same transcendent experience.

The five pillars of Islam support a people dedicated to God. The *shahada* is the pole around which the essence of the Muslim faith—the transcendent experience of God—rotates. The other four pillars set in motion the surrender—prayer five times a day, almsgiving, fasting at Ramadan, and the pilgrimage to Mecca. The formula is ingenious and holds a diverse people together while compelling individuals to perform this duty of right living and sharing with others.

CHAPTER FOUR

Insights into Islam

⌁

The Origin of Islam in the Desert

There have been a few themes that have emerged in the Muslim–Catholic dialogue that have given me insight into Islam. The first insight I have had is the shaping of Islam by its origins in the desert, which I talked briefly about at the end of the previous chapter. Muhammad was a merchant and not a nomad, but he spent a great deal of time alone in the desert and in caravans, crossing its great expanse. While Islam has appealed to the many cultures of the cities and towns in mountains and forests, I believe that its origins in the vastness of a desert and the scarcity of water, food, and shelter created an archetypal psyche that had to be tough enough to "make do," to make sacrifices, and to defer comfort. It encouraged thinking ahead, planning, and using things in moderation, because what was at stake was not comfort and more ease but life or death.

In addition, there were the distances that needed to be traveled with few people around to help. Much

effort was required to get from point to point trans-
porting goods to barter with someone. Because of the
threat of raids on one's caravan, there were strong
incentives to bond together against common foes, to
trust another's word, and to count on a deal—all of
which was offset against the vulnerability of being
isolated because and for the sake of the harsh and
unrelenting climate. The desert is fierce and only the
strong can negotiate it. As with Tibetans in their
mountainous terrain, one can assume that only the
hardiest of Arab offspring, well adapted to live in such
conditions, would survive. While the Islamic faith
grew and absorbed non-desert-dwelling peoples such
as Europeans, Africans, Asians and Americans, the
origin of this religion has the strength of the desert. By
thinking of Islam in this way—as a religion conceived
in and toughened by the desert—we can see how it has
endured from generation to generation and from
country to country. It had built-in adaptation mecha-
nisms and traveled fast and light—not weighed down
by doctrinal baggage, political superstructure, or
symbolic overload: the perfect mode for traveling
safely in the desert.

We might be so bold as to say that the desert does
for the Muslims what the cross does for Christians—
it unifies contradictions and saves. Its barrenness
confronts one directly with God, without mediation
or representation. The oases offer visions of heaven,

and mirages demand that one be aware of illusion. The arc of the horizon forms a slow crescent moon, while the stars in the cloudless night sky above provide evidence of the miracle of creation and the necessary humility required to surrender to it. The starkness of the surrounding space opens up the opportunity for the transcendent God to fill it with all-merciful love.

In Indiana, we have four annual seasons of almost equal length. To me, the desert calls forth an abiding inner place beneath the flow of ordinary consciousness. It has its seasons, too, but its changes strike me as ancient and slow-moving, hidden and mysterious, but somehow *known* by us in our hearts. It helps me to understand Islam by thinking of it as the terrain of a desert, crossed by caravans that direct themselves solely toward God.

An Unmediated Symbol System

Islam provides a cohesive grid of inner strength using an unmediated symbol system. A social scientist might have crisper language to describe this insight, but as I sit at the table of dialogue with my Muslim friends I catch their three-dimensional faith: "There is no God but God; I surrender in awe, bending my knee and bowing my head; upon rising I live with others according to the Qur'an." Muslims, as people of the revelation of God spoken through the Qur'an, have a

direct access to God through hearing those inspired
words mediated by Muhammad.

One weekday morning a few years ago, Judith
Cebula, religion reporter for the *Indianapolis Star*,
interviewed Dr. Shahid Athar and his wife and myself
for an article on women in Catholicism and Islam.
Judith asked us why Islam was so attractive and was
the fastest-growing religion in the world. I said that as
a catechist I admired the clarity of Islam; it was simply
an easier religion to teach, even though it was prob-
ably harder to live by. Dr. Athar was surprised at my
statement and asked me why I thought Islam was so
catechetically appealing. I told him that Catholicism
has at its heart the teaching of the Trinity—Jesus, the
Son of God, sent by the Father and leaving us with the
love of the Holy Spirit. In Islam, I noted, there is One
God, who provided a revelation mediated by the
Prophet Muhammad. There is no mediation of the
Church of Christ, but direct worship, duty, and way
of faith. While Islam is complex, sophisticated, and
multi-layered in its history, context, scholars, and
teachers, and in its vast array of color and texture
because of its size, many cultures, and artistic achieve-
ments, the faith system is still direct, immediate,
personal, and specific.

Islam's particular focus has been mediation with
God through the possessions of this world. In Islam
there do not exist the "other worldly" sacraments

such as the seven sacraments of Catholics (baptism, confirmation, Eucharist, penance, matrimony, last rites, and ordination to the priesthood) or other signs and symbols of the blessing of God. Like Jews, Muslims receive God's blessings through material prosperity as signs of approval and approbation. This is not something unique to monotheism. Hindus also pray to Lakshmi, the goddess of wealth and prosperity, and the Tibetans to Vasudhara. The link with prosperity in Christianity is most often seen in Protestantism, but Catholicism has certainly throughout its history often raised the acquisition of material wealth to a visible level of opulence. At one time, the Roman Church owned much of the territory of Europe. Monastics in my own tradition became landowners and aristocratic power brokers. All monotheistic religions believe at their core that if God is good, then goodness follows. In Christianity, however, the corrective to the acquisition of wealth is that it is better to renounce than to be weighted down with material goods, while in Islam, as we have seen, there is an egalitarianism that governs economic wellbeing for even the poorest of its members.

At one of the first Muslim–Catholic dialogues hosted at the Islamic Society of North America, I asked if there were a video that would be good to view to learn more about Islam. I was given a video that said, "Islam is economic ascendancy under

Allah." The sacrament for Muslims is an economic
order where justice prevails, the poor are cared for,
and there is peace and wellbeing. There is no separation of Church and State. It is here, it seems to me,
that the "this worldly" dimension needs to be
grasped—that it is in *this* world that people surrender
to God. Good will be rewarded both now and in eternity—a reward that comes directly from God and not
through symbolic gestures or ritual sacraments. Earth
is a sacrament and ordinary life is the Islamic way of
salvation. Blessings are material and visible signs of
God's favor (See *Islam: The Story of Islam*).

When Muslims call Christians infidels, they are not
complaining so much about our being unfaithful to
doctrines about God as much as our failing to pursue
the economic justice that is God's imperative for
followers. With an unmediated symbol system (which
means no Jesus Christ), there is naked presence
between the transcendent God and the human's right
living (righteousness). Consequent to my experience of
dialogue with Islam, I have had to ask myself if I have
misused my belief in Jesus, my Lord, in neglecting my
part in helping others live. In one sense, there is no
need for the separation of Church and State, as there is
no Church to be distinct from. In Islam there is no
middle term—only Allah and the People of God. There
is also no "State," if we see the state as a person or
group that can make decisions independently of God,

because there is no secular, freestanding anything. All is under Allah. Allah blesses humans with the Earth and all its gifts. This understanding operates as the center of gravity for all political zones.

An extreme manifestation of this identity may be operating in Iran, which is ruled by clerics. Iran does not, as far as I am concerned, represent the natural or ultimate expression of the faithful Islamic state—given that there are faithful Muslims who live in all the democracies. Iran is more of a historical accident—rather like Christendom when it was governed under the Divine Right of Kings and when such religio-political entities as the Holy Roman Empire and the Papal States existed. The deeper point I now understand is that Islam's way of life is non-hierarchical and its wealth comes about as an expression of God's favor, in a way that is similar to the Jewish identification of "favor" through wealth. That can be in any nation or country; it is only the fundamentalist Jewish stream that insists on the historic property known as Israel with its center city, Jerusalem; and it is only fundamentalist Muslims that insist on Islamic "rule." A Christianity that follows Jesus' directives is neither political nor economic. Instead, it sees the reign of God as not of this world; we live here humanly engaged, neither needing to rule politically nor with prosperity or physical wealth sanctifying our lives.

Ascendancy View

What do I mean by "ascendancy" in the previous section? For Muslims, Islam is the one true faith in that it is the last revelation of the God of Abraham, Moses, and Jesus. Through Muhammad, Muslims believe, the Islamic tradition of surrender is the fullest expression of belief, the direct way to God, and the perfect relationship.

When participating in a meeting in Chicago, I visited a Bahai Temple in Wilmette, Illinois. The white, Persian architecture of a perfect temple to the heavens lifted my spirits and I delighted in its beauty. We came to the gathering space beneath the prayer hall to the welcoming center. There was a wall-sized histogram that plotted time from Adam, Abraham, Moses, Jesus, Muhammad, and, in the largest, boldest, graphic, Bahaullah, the Persian founder of Bahai. In this case, all previous revelations were incorporated into the one great religious truth of the Kitab-I-Izan, "The Book of Certitude," of the Bahai faith. This graphic of ascendancy made my heart sink. I felt that Jesus the Christ was just a subset of this faith and not the Way, the Truth, and the Light. If a Muslim had entered that welcome center, she or he would have had the same sinking feeling. The Prophet Muhammad was just one more prophet in the line of other distinguished prophets, who were all superseded and subsumed under the wings of the final prophet,

Bahaullah of the Bahai. Since then, I have been in many dialogues that eventually come to this same impasse—each religion thinks of itself as the final and complete message of salvation. Father Bruno Barnhart, a monk at the Monastery of New Camaldoli in Big Sur, California, says that each religion fills out the entire landscape. It is natural to see history from our own point of view. We are not God.

Bernard Lewis picks a middle way between triumphalism and relativism when he says that human beings may use different religions to speak to God, as they use different languages to speak to one another, but that God understands them all (see Lewis, p. 39). From a dialogue point of view, I find it is helpful to speak my own experience and listen to my dialogue partner without judgment. The content is persons, not God. God can take care of Himself! Though revelation is certain, dogmas change with understanding and growth.

In a little book such as this, there is no place for an extended analysis of the sense of ascendancy that devotees of many faiths feel of their own faith. All adherents have an identity forged through their particular faith, which, at some level, makes it necessary for them to relate to another faith in a particular way. This is perhaps a function of human nature, a way to feel wholehearted in one's commitment. Feeling that sense of ascendancy creates solidarity, a sense of belonging and yet of being apart from others. Unfortunately, throughout human history, this feeling of ascendancy has had a negative side—which is to see the non-member of one's religion as someone who does not "belong" and is on a road to perdition unless he or she is saved. All religions, therefore, to some degree have a natural tendency to share their message and integrate it into society—what we Christians mean by "evangelize." Such an attitude, however, can leave no oxygen for others who have different beliefs to breathe.

Because of its sense of ascendancy, Islam has, like Christianity, undergone crisis after crisis. What makes Islam particularly vulnerable to the negative dimensions of a belief in ascendancy is the belief in God without division as well as the idea that it is in this lifetime that we will be blessed, as opposed to dwelling on the spiritual benefits of the life beyond. Therefore, ascendancy that is both economic, political, and theological is on a collision course with other faiths and cultures. What all religious practitioners need to understand—especially religions that emphasize that their way of practice is "the Way, the Truth, and the Life"—is that, as I say earlier, religion is not God. God is more than any religion. Religion is a human system for the human effort at relating to God. Consequently, it cannot be perfect and unique. In fact, some religious writers distinguish their faith tradition (be it Christianity, Buddhism, Islam, or whatever) from religion as a human institution. The truth that Islamic ascendancy asserts is that God is and God is One. Other considerations need not detract from the pure form of God-consciousness.

Muslims believe God revealed to Muhammad a way to reconnect with our Creator through the path of surrender. That sense of surrender in and of itself offers a sense of ascendancy that in its totality is profound and profoundly meaningful. However, such a sense cannot be used as a template for "others." Extremists within Islam take the economic and theological sense of ascendancy as a literal truth that they wish to apply to all members and nonmembers of their faith. Moderate Muslims, particularly here in the United States, see their Islam as a personal practice that supports their work for self-determination. They experience the complexity of relating to a secular culture and maintaining their faith.

I should emphasize here that in none of our Muslim–Catholic dialogue sessions has there been anything but respect for the distinctions and differences between Islam and Catholicism expressed by either myself or my dialogists. We all feel energy and delight in getting to know and appreciating each other as the "other." What the United States offers my Muslim friends, many of whom are first-generation immigrants, as well as those who were born here seems to be the possibility of healthy pluralism. Living side by side with people of different cultural and religious backgrounds and working together with them on common "goods" for families, neighborhoods, country, and the world is one of America's great gifts. Islam, as a global religion, has always had to negotiate with other religions, and in America it is negotiating its place in a democratic culture. The events of September 11, 2001, and other so-called Islamic terrorist activity before and since come out of a brand of Islam that is deeply alien to the vast majority of Muslims, just as the kind of evangelical Christianity that argues that one will go to Hell unless one is born again and that all non-Christians will go to hell for all eternity is deeply embarrassing to the vast majority of Christians. Unfortunately, fundamentalism manifests itself in all our religions, and it is always a source of conflict. I agree with Dr. Athar when he says that a religion cannot be judged by the behavior or wrong actions of those who claim to be born in that faith but who practice the opposite of what the faith teaches. In the next chapter, I attempt to address the three questions most often asked of me by non-Muslims reacting to Islam in the world today.

CHAPTER FIVE

Three Questions

Over the seven years of dialogue my Muslim friends and I have had many technical conversations about the Bible and the Qur'an, the Prophet, and Jesus Christ, the expectations of the afterlife, the moral codes, and so forth. However, three themes have emerged, mostly from the Catholic side, that have begged for clarification: fundamentalism, women's rights, and democratic principles.

1. Does Islam foster violent fundamentalism?

When people in the West talk about "Islamic fundamentalism," they are generally thinking of the very strict versions of Islam that seem to them to encourage martyrdom and foster highly repressive laws, especially for women. They are thinking of the kind of the Wahhabi-oriented Islam of Osama bin Laden and women covered from head to toe in clothing that makes it difficult for them to see or move around. They are thinking of the woman who was accused of having a child out of wedlock and was sentenced to death by stoning by an Islamic court in northern Nigeria, using a strict interpretation of *shari'a* law.

They are thinking of the girls who are not allowed to go to school in Afghanistan or the women who are not allowed to drive in Saudi Arabia. Unfortunately, Christians themselves could detail story after story of the misguided zeal of fundamentalist and reactionary behaviors—from bombing abortion clinics to withholding medicine from a dying child, from expelling a pregnant adolescent girl from secondary school to Christian polygamy in Utah.

Muslims and Christians alike are appalled by the Christian leaders that liken Islam to Satanism.[1] Such hatred of another seems to be more than simple ignorance. Likewise, the Jungian theory that all of us have a "shadow" side that acts out unless integrated into the personality, or the stories about demons in our own scriptures, are inadequate as explanations of the disproportionate damage done to the innocent by these cruel and unfeeling actions. The Desert Fathers, speaking from experience, declare that those who judge others actually nourish the seeds of that same manifestation of evil in themselves, and that the more they judge others, the more vulnerable they are to the same sin that the accusers accuse the "other" of committing. The speck in the other's eye really *is* the beam in their own.

In a dialogue on purity of heart at New Camaldoli Monastery in Big Sur, Father William Skudlarek of St. John's Abbey wrote a paper on *zazen* entitled "A Path from Judgment to Love." He took the meaning of the Desert Fathers even deeper: Jesus' words on not judging, he said, were not about the subject or object of one's judgment. If a practitioner judges, that practitioner is not a practitioner. We must love with the same love that God loves us in Jesus (see Skudlarek, p. 149).

I will never forget one particular session of Muslim–Catholic dialogue just days after September 11, 2001, when several of us gathered together to discuss what had happened. We were from India, Pakistan, Iran, and Palestine, now living in St. Louis, Detroit, Toledo, Louisville, Indianapolis, Chicago, and Washington, DC. The Muslims recounted story after story of anti-Muslim retaliation, balanced by warm letters they had received from Catholic school-children, as well as visits and donations. When the Muslims' windows had been smashed, Christians had come over to help mend them, and in so doing had mended more than windows. I could feel the dense sadness and protracted silence that lay within our common heart and between our shared tears. American dreams had been shattered. We went on with our work collaborating on a paper on God's Word and the word of God.

Fundamentalist adherents seem to be clustered in small or large groups who feel rejected by their own membership. As believers they feel strongly, indeed passionately, about their faith and are zealous in practicing the required duties. They tend to accept the revelation, the law, or the customs associated with their faith literally, with no interpretation other than their own. Their aim is to move from making themselves and their associates more faithful to their faith's message of peace and worship to converting unbelievers. When their efforts are rebuffed, the zeal coalesces into rage, and rage begets violence as the fundamentalist seeks to get the "other" to conform. To the extent that the beliefs and practices of Islam are clear and there is a strong tendency toward both material and theological ascendancy, fundamentalism as a fanatical force can have room to develop.

In one of our Buddhist–Catholic dialogues a monk called me to say that he was not able to come because an evangelical Protestant missionary group was proselytizing in his village in Burma, and his family had asked him to come home to stop the persecution of Buddhists by Christians in their town. Christians were burning Buddhist homes and businesses. There are far too many examples in history of violence caused by religious zeal. Catholics still blush with shame at the Crusades, the horrors of the Inquisition, and our tacit approval of Jewish persecution in Europe, which culminated in the Holocaust. In 1992, Monastic Interreligious Dialogue forged a declaration, signed by many religious leaders, that religion can no longer be used as a reason for war. The Church, especially through the many visits of the late Pope John Paul II, has been indefatigable on behalf of reconciliation.

One of the monks who was deeply involved in Catholic–Muslim relations was the Superior at the Trappist Monastery of Atlas in Algiers, where, in June 1996, five Christian monks were abducted and beheaded. Abbot Armand Veilleux accompanied the Trappist Superior General to Algiers from Rome to identify the bodies of the slain monks. When I asked the abbot if he thought Islam was a religion that had core beliefs that led to violence, he told me the following:

> What did I learn about Islam in the contacts I had with Muslims? I think I would stress the fact that the "normal" Muslim is a deeply religious and usually peace-loving person. Fanaticism and terrorism are not representative of the Muslim world and certainly not of Islam. They are representative of a small percentage of Muslims. And we should add these Muslims are pushed towards fanaticism by the aggression and the unfairness of the Western countries. When people are deprived of their rights,

are humiliated and left without any hope for a
better future, recourse to violence is almost
unavoidable.[2]

Abbot Armand's response forced me to think
about my own faith. Did Catholicism, at its core,
foster violence in the name of its faith? I sincerely
believe that the answer is "no." Both Catholicism and
Islam have, at their core, teachings concerning peace
and harmony among all nations. Both Islam and
Catholicism have to travel the journey of faith toward
their own way, truth, and life, and not fight to destroy
the "other" ways of reaching that goal.

I have learned in the Muslim–Catholic dialogue
that Islam has a rich tradition of right action and
training in ethics not unlike Buddhism. Dr. Athar, a
physician, has a strong teaching on "lying" as a
disease of the spiritual heart:

Lying is against human nature, against physi-
ology, and, like a disease, has its own signs and
symptoms. The act of lying produces inner
conflicts between various control centers of the
brain. The moment one begins to lie, the body
sends out contradictory signals to cause facial
muscle twitching, expansion and contraction
of pupils, perspiration, flushing of cheeks,
increased eye blinking, tremor of hand, and

rapid heart rate. These constitute the basis of lie-detector instruments. In addition, you will notice the liar is unconsciously doing some movements like covering his mouth, nose touching, eye rubbing, scratching the side of the neck, cupping his ear, etc. One of the clearest signs is that the liar keeps his palms closed and eyes pointed to another direction rather than facing the person eye to eye when he is lying. A liar is aware of his body signals, therefore he finds lying easier when no one can see him, i.e., on the phone or in writing.

Dr. Athar goes on to discuss motives for lying—if it is ever justified—and the value of truth: "Truthfulness is a command of God, part of faith, and an essential quality for all prophets and is mentioned in one hundred places in the Qur'an" (Athar, p. 202).

Violence is like lying. It is my understanding of Islam that not only are Muslims offended by the "bad zeal" of fundamentalist groups, but they are striving for ethical personal practices with good zeal that would make all of us saints if we followed the directives of the Qur'an.

2. What about women's equality?

Another question that constantly occurs in Muslim–Catholic dialogue is whether Islam is inherently opposed to women's equality with men or can we attribute the apparent oppression of women to a cultural time lag? This question is one that we Catholic women also pose to our Church leaders— usually around the sticking point of ordination to the priesthood. In my experience, many women religious and lay believers question the theological reason why women cannot be ordained in the Roman rite (that Jesus did not appoint any women among his twelve disciples). They feel that the reason is more cultural than theological. I personally do not feel called to be ordained to the priesthood; but I respect deeply those men and women who do, and I feel that Catholics would be served well and well served by women priests, as well as they are now being served by married priests who have converted to Catholicism. This opinion, I should add, is not confined to my fellow women religious. Most of my male priest friends and associates state the same preference.

It is my belief that in time the Vatican will soften on this issue and that more married men and women will be ordained—the aging of the celibate male priesthood and the devotion and energy of women will make it both a necessity and a great source of joy and vigor for the Church. The issue of gender as a requirement for ordination is for me one governed by history, and, like most historical issues, this one will be resolved over time. The obstacles will fall away

and the reasons that were used in support of discipli-
nary action or doctrinal rigidity will fall away as
well.

I suspect that the issues that some women have
regarding their role in Islam could stem from the same
cultural time sequence. In my dialogue sessions with
Muslims, men and women come together. From
informal talks I have had with the women, I have
learned how each country of their countries of origin
has a range of observances that govern the role, dress,
and functions of women. There are liberal and conservative groups within each country, although women
are emerging as autonomous and powerful presences
in all countries around the world. There are Muslim
organizations working on behalf of women and
supporting their struggles around the world. Just as
there is no spokesperson representing all Catholic
women, so there is no unified voice for Muslim
women.

In all societies and countries throughout the
world, women's roles are changing. Less and less is
marriage viewed as a tidy partnership that demands a
wife's unquestioning submission to her husband or a
husband's absolute domination of his wife. Children
raised today do not automatically have the same
values of their parents. This transition for many societies, both Muslim and non-Muslim, can be difficult.

Is it harder, however, for Muslim women to

change? Is there anything intrinsic to Islam that
curtails women's freedom?

To a degree, the answer has to be no. Women's
lives throughout history and under many different
faith practices have been extraordinarily difficult.
Even today, women and children make up the
majority of the world's poor, and forced marriages
and lack of access to health care for bringing children
into this world are still widespread throughout the
world. We need to remember that Christianity was,
quite literally, brought into the world through a pregnant, unwed teenager, Mary—a plight mirrored in
countless young women's lives around the globe.

That said—and this is only the opinion of a nun,
and an opinion offered humbly—I feel that Islam grew
up in a culture of toughness that will only soften its
edges as it applies its own values of egalitarian principles to gender roles.[3]

The fact of the desert, the direct access to God
without mediation of symbols, and a rigorous prayer
life both in public and in the home that is male-
dominated gives me the impression that women will
need special affirmation to be equal partners. Islam
spread through conquest and consolidation, with an
emphasis on education, feats of arms, and an
assembly at prayer that, even today, does not allow
women in the main area of the mosque. Nevertheless, Islam places a special emphasis on the protec-

tion and care of, as well as respect for, women. Indeed, Muhammad took the lead in insisting on a woman's right to divorce, the possession of property, and the learning of the Qur'an (admittedly at home and under the guidance of men) (see Armstrong, *Muhammad*, p. 198). Unlike in Christianity, there are no images of God, male or female, so God is not automatically viewed as an old man with a white beard. That said, it is the man rather than the woman who is assumed to be the leader of the family under God.

Change, when it happens, can happen quickly. When I grew up in the 1950s, my father and his brothers went into business together. My father's four sisters were excluded from the partnership. My siblings went to Catholic schools from first grade through college and my mother thought of no work other than being a homemaker. My father led the rosary and the meal prayers, drove the car, and passed his business on to his oldest son. Nowadays, this is changing, and the gender roles are blurring. It is not surprising that immigrant families from Asia and the Middle East moving to America or Europe experience culture shock.

In monastic orders, things are also changing. When I entered the convent in September 1961, I was given the long black skirt and short veil of a postulant. By May 1962, I was invested with the traditional

black wool serge habit and a veil that extended to the
back of my knees. I had a coif that covered my face, a
dress dating back to the ninth century that went to the
floor, and sleeves that amply covered all but my
hands. I wore this or its modifications for almost fourteen years. I think that it is highly problematic for men
to dictate a woman's dress. While I felt happy wearing
an identifying garment that expressed my vowed life,
I also felt that the black habit was a barrier between
me and the students I taught.

Most women in the "developed" world are
appalled by what they see as the "control" of women
in the "undeveloped" world; although it would be
worth examining our own "developed" assumptions
about the "freedom" given to women through
fashion, advertising, and pornography. What
"Western" women do not take account of, however, is
that there are some women who *choose* to wear the
hijab for symbolic and safety reasons. Throughout the
centuries and in all countries, clothes (except, it often
seems, in ritual) change and adapt to the times. I do
not wear the veil today because to me it says more
about division and disdain for the human community
than it does about reverence for the awesome vocation
to religious vows.

Women are represented in Islam in other ways. In
her work on women and Islam, scholar Annemarie
Schimmel has emphasized the feminine dimension of

Islam through the Sufi poems of the female mystic Rabia, the Turkish poet Rumi, and others.

I feel I have an affinity with Sufi devotees. Their practices have heightened God-consciousness and have inspired some of the greatest religious poetry and music ever written. When I am with Sufis and participate in the prayer to our same God, I feel their intensity. Some of that intensity's exuberance seems more like the Christian charismatic movements than the low-key, everyday chant of the monastic choir. Nevertheless, the sober phases of Sufism seem like a great "fit" with my own love for Our Lord, Jesus Christ—through our daily inner conversations. Sufism is a way of love (see Ernst).

Sufism shares with monasticism a course that runs counter to fundamentalist approaches to religion. This is because the mystical experience repeatedly transcends doctrinal and institutional policies. Both Sufism and monasticism are happily marginal to mainstream society. Some prefer to use the word *liminal*—as in "crossing the threshold"—to describe the movement to a contemplative way of life both inside and out revealed in these practices. Whatever the phrase, the way of love goes to the heart of spiritual practice.

I have been warmed by the mysticism of the heart present in Sufism. As I prepared for the dialogue on "Purity of Heart" held in 2000, a dialogue between a

Sufi and Thomas Merton, the great Trappist scholar
and instigator of interreligious dialogue, caught my
attention—as a woman and practitioner with a deep
sense of the feminine (see Wong and Barnhart). In his
reflections on the contemplative life, Merton talks of
le point vierge, a place of absolute purity—a spotless
spot, as it were—untouchable by sin. Although the
metaphor of the virginal point naturally has a sexual
component, the concept transcends sexuality or
gender. While *le point vierge* is indeed a place of
conception and inception, where the mystery of life
meets the miracle of birth, *le point vierge* is, more
completely, the central point where, in apparent
despair, one meets God and is found completely in His
mercy (see Baker and Henry, p. 64). It is a profoundly
pure meeting-point—essential, sinless, forever new. I
believe that Sufism offers a similar point of purity in
its heart-centered practice. The word *devotion* is
sometimes denigrated as denoting a superficial or irra-
tional form of worship; but Sufi devotion, I feel,
makes a deep avowal to life with God—an avowal as
sacred as a marriage between partners.

Sufis practice what is known as the "science of
hearts." Sufism began its development of Islamic
mysticism by identifying anomalies in the spiritual life
of the believer who prays and who must be simple and
naked. This analysis served to designate the errors of
judgment, the mental pretenses, and the hypocrisies of

the spiritual life—thus tearing away the barriers between the devotee and God. In this instance, the "heart" represents the incessant oscillation of the human will that beats under the impulse of various passions, an impulse that must be stabilized by the Essential Desire, the One God. Introspection must guide us to tear through the concentric "veils" that ensheath the heart and hide from us the immaculate or virginal point (*le point vierge*) or, in Sufi terms, the secret (*sirr*), wherein God manifests Himself (see Baker and Henry, p. 66).

I, myself, have also found a sense of the feminine in Islam's wonderful teachings on angels. In Islam, the devout feel the presence of angels everywhere!

For the most part, Islam's cultural patterns and religious values are tightly woven and women are as bound to their position in their cultures as men are. It is often easier to stay in a constrained situation that you know than to seek the freedom of true equality—for both men and women—in a way that is unfamiliar. This is not something unique to Islam or the cultures in which Islam has flourished. I am an American woman and, in spite of the great strides made by women over the last century, I can attest that I am still not an equal partner in many aspects of my life with a man. As I watch my nieces grow into women I see this changing in a natural, mutually positive way.

None of this cultural conditioning and time-bounded-ness should be surprising. Religion binds things together in negative as well as positive ways. It gathers the values of the society, in which it is practiced and stores the archives of the history of the religion in that society and tries to make both relevant for the next generation. The challenge is to make the classic memories and trusted practices of generations ago accessible to the contemporary members of society without forcing them to live in the past. Where all of us need to be vigilant is in not allowing oppression and repression to occur in our respective religious traditions through those in power falling back on expressions such as "God said so," simply to maintain their cultural and political dominance. God is beyond such petty political maneuvering.

It is a contention of the women's movement in the United States that the oppression of women is the oppression of men, too. It is time-consuming and enervating to try to control everything about your world, including the practice of others who simply share similar enthusiasms and a love of God. We women religious believe that men should be relieved of some of the burden of their responsibility and share in the joy, honor, and responsibility of being worshipers and celebrants of God. None of us should use our religion to justify the oppression of women— whether Muslim or Christian, Buddhist or Jew. Additionally, from a spiritual point of view, there is a benefit in transcending gender-consciousness to lead to God-consciousness. That transcendence exerts compassion for all, regardless of gender, race, nationality, rank, or geographic boundaries. After all, awareness of gender can be manipulated through simply transferring domination from one gender to another or retaliating angrily. Sometimes we all need to practice humility and charity rather than stridency or making demands. Civility and a sincere wish for the other's benefit are both the content and process of dialogue at its best.

3. Can Islam be democratic?

Finally, we need to ask about whether Islam can adapt to democratic principles. The simplest answer is, yes, it can. Turkey is almost wholly Islamic and it is a democracy, although there have been a number of coups over the years by a military fiercely dedicated to making sure that the state is secular, and there remains a troubling abuse of human rights, especially against the Kurdish minority. Indonesia, a majority Muslim country, after years of brutal dictatorship, is now a democracy, although anti-Christian and anti-Chinese riots are a disturbing reality and the country is far from stable. The world's largest democracy, India, has a population of over 120 million Muslims. Muslims have enjoyed representation in Parliament since independence, although the power

of the Hindu nationalist Bharatiya Janata Party or
BJP is at the time of this writing cause for concern,
and the sporadic fighting between Hindus and
Muslims in parts of India, as well as the tension
between India and Pakistan, continue to pose grave
problems. It is worth noting that democratic Muslim
countries have seen several women prime ministers:
the late Benazir Bhutto in then-democratic Pakistan,
Megawati Sukarnoputri in today's Indonesia, Begum
Khaleda Zia in Bangladesh in 1991 and Sheikh
Hasina Wajed in 1996, and Tansu Çiller in Turkey in
the mid-1990s.

The issue, therefore, is not whether Islam can
adapt to democracy, but whether Islam can live
comfortably in a pluralistic and secular society that
uniformly respects human rights and the rule of law
but does not privilege any religion in its law or media.
Again, I see no reason why this cannot happen—it is
happening throughout Europe and in the United
States, where many Muslims have thrived. Muslims
have taken on leadership positions in many communities throughout the world, winning election to city
councils, regional boards, and even in parliaments
throughout Europe. Their educational discipline and
business acumen have given Muslims opportunities to
lift a whole population: the renaissance of the town of
Leicester in the British Midlands, for instance, has
often been credited to the influx of many South Asian

Muslims who renovated houses and brought back businesses long lost to urban blight.

The challenge Muslims face is the challenge that all religious practitioners in Western democracies have had to face—to recognize the right of "others" to practice their faith and to acknowledge that another person's practice of faith is as true to him or her as their own is to them. No religion *can* be the dominant way to God. A theocracy cannot sustain pluralistic values: it is simply a contradiction in terms. We Catholics have had difficulty finding language that says how we feel: we love Jesus Christ and are confident in our salvation though Christ. All the various ways of sharing this belief risk being a judgment of another's path. I have come to the realization that Islam *is*, it just *is*, and we Catholics can wholeheartedly appreciate it as a means to God. From the original points of our initiations into faith we can live side by side, living fully as Christians and Muslims in a family larger than each of us and all of us put together.

Ironically, it has been dialogue with Buddhists that has helped me with a measured language about God. One of St. Benedict's teachers, John Cassian of the fourth century, spoke of renunciation of our "thought" of God because any "thought" is not God, but a human action. Therefore, at the deepest level of my heart I have to renounce my "thought" of God, because that thought is not God. In other words, I must learn to let God be God. It is this profound mystery and deep reverence that I place before my Muslim friends as they speak wholeheartedly to their One God beyond all names. Can we live on the same planet with the same earth under our feet and the name of the same God of the heavens as we see it? I certainly think we can.

At a meeting held at Gethsemani Abbey in Kentucky in April 2002, an event known as "Gethsemani Encounter II," Fordham University professor of theology Father Leo Lefebure challenged the Christians among us to get beyond a narrow theism that makes "God" look bad.[4] God, he told us, cannot be a function of our ego, nor can it be a wedge for divisions and oppression. As the great medieval German mystic Meister Eckhart would have it, God is really "not-God" because we, God's creatures, are not the proper ones to "define" Him—if we were, we would be God! To me, in the face of this mystery, silence and adoration, or the bow of the Muslim five times a day, are the proper gesture.

In helping Islam adapt itself to the postmodern, postindustrial, globalized world of pluralistic culture and individualized faith, it is important that the West take very seriously the effect of its own secularism on people of faith, wherever they may come from. Since September 11, 2001, and the attack on the Pentagon and the World Trade Center, the United States and other majority non-Muslim nations have had to try to understand Islam from the ground up. Our ignorance has been revealed to us and our intolerance has not been attractive. Our common goal as Muslims and Christians has to be the instillation of the best of democracy in all our hearts. We must begin to dialogue about what is just or unjust aggression and out of what sense of humiliation come the horrors of terrorism. (In Louay M. Safi's *Peace and the Limits of War: Transcending Classical Conception of Jihad* we have a clear teaching on the Islamic notion of war and peace written after September 11).[5] I have appreciated the cautionary words of Dr. Hassan Hathout, Director of Outreach at the Islamic Center of Southern California. Just like communism, says Dr. Hathout, capitalism is inherently materialistic. Democracy can just be another oppressive ideology that substitutes individualism and risks the common good. Western culture's biggest threat to humankind is materialism and self-seeking (see Hathout).

Catholicism and Islam share a similar vision of themselves as religions of peace. We have both learned in our long and uncomfortable history of confrontation and mutual disregard that violence begets violence. We both know that in our objectification and vilification of the "other" we take on the worst aspects of the one we hate. Americans cannot

insist on democracy that has an agenda of forwarding
only their own economic interests. Islamic countries
must acknowledge individual rights and practice
tolerance for, as well as safeguard in law, the right to
free speech and assembly. All societies must condemn
all acts of terrorism. Neither Islamic nor Christian
political leaders should establish an agenda in which
the one is defined as "good" and the "other" is
defined as "evil." This is for God to decide. God
respects the free will of choice based on the individual's conscience. To put it another way, oppression
is oppression whatever part of the religious or political spectrum it comes from.

Is there an answer to the tyranny of theocratic,
economic, and ideological ascendancy? I believe that
there is—and the answer is dialogue. Catholics are
just now beginning to learn the lesson that we can
affirm the truth, beauty, and goodness of faith wherever we meet it. Through dialogue, we are beginning
to understand the great wisdom traditions of the
world and are finding ourselves surprised and
delighted by similarities as well as challenged and
deepened by differences. We are acknowledging that
while we may never understand the full *richness* of the
other's religion, we all have a deep commitment to the
poor, who can teach us how to love and be loving as
a way of life.

CHAPTER SIX

Conclusion

In this little book I have tried to present a clear picture of Islam for Western minds with open hearts. I appreciate the five pillars as ingenious practices that make Islam a great religion, and I can see why so many accept their good example and become Muslim. I have outlined four traits of Islam not as hard-and-fast truths but as insights that have helped me understand where a Muslim dialogue partner is coming from.

My journey of understanding is just beginning. I intend to learn more about the Holy Prophet Muhammad and the sacred revelation of the Qur'an. I hope to study further the origins of Islam, founded by Muhammad from his desert home. I have argued that Islam has a cohesiveness that is unmediated by sign and symbol other than the five pillars and the way of life taught in the Qur'an, and that Christians would better understand Islam if we took note of the Muslim belief in sacramentality embedded in earthly prosperity. I have also suggested that Christians need

to be fully aware of the Muslim belief in the sacredness of the Qur'an and Muhammad as the final and
last prophet. And, lastly, I have looked at three
controversial questions regarding Islam—fundamentalism, women's equality, and the democratic poten-
tial of Islamic states. I know that I have simply intro-
duced and certainly not resolved these issues, but I
wanted to share how these issues are spoken of with
courage and candor at the table of the scholars,
imams, physicians, nuns, priests, bishops, theologians,
and scholars with whom I have been in dialogue. That
these questions can be raised at all is because my
Muslim friends are not afraid to speak to these issues
with wit and wisdom. When we *know* and *respect*
each other, this kind of face-to-face dialogue becomes
human and natural and beautiful.

Who, therefore, is a Muslim? A Muslim is
someone who believes that there is no God but Allah,
and that Muhammad is Allah's messenger—it is that
simple and that direct. The Muslim sees the imprint of
God in everything and everyone because we are all
God's creatures. Through the pillars of the practice of
his or her faith, the Muslim expresses his or her belief
in God and in so doing joins him- or herself to all
other believers who submit to Allah.

A Muslim is bound to give money to the poor, but
he does not renounce wealth. He fasts for one month
and does not eat pork, but eats normally the other

eleven months of the year. A Muslim is obligated to make a pilgrimage to Mecca at least once in his lifetime; but if he is unable to go through sickness or poverty he can perform charitable acts at home. A Muslim bows five times a day to Allah and recites the prayers from his heart day in and day out, whether alone or with other Muslims, from morning until bedtime, punctuating the day with prayer inspired by faith. A Muslim knows the Qur'an, the customs and laws, and follows them wholeheartedly in this world with eager expectations of eternal life.

Islam in this regard is not a set of precepts to aspire to or a set of symbols of perfection. Islam is a lived and earthly existence governed by a direct connection to God in a life of surrender. Islam is a revealed pattern of being human that exists to create order from chaos—which is perhaps why Islamic culture has so often excelled in mathematics and science, architecture and calligraphy.

Some may feel that it is strange that I should argue, as I have in this book, that Islam, a most earthly religion, is nevertheless a fully formed vehicle toward God-consciousness. Islam is, indeed, earthly. The five pillars combined knot each human forehead to the earth five times a day before God's mercy, gathering the people of God together every day and then, in a ritual of origin, once in a lifetime at Mecca. By calling the faithful to Mecca, Islam allows each

Muslim to be embodied historically in a place and demands that each Muslim share financial and physical blessings with the poor. The Muslim recites the creed from what I like to call a memorized heart—where the inspiration and expiration of God through the repetition of the fact of the one God and Muhammad, His messenger, operates like the systole and diastole of the heart. Likewise, through the Halal laws and the period of Ramadan, the Muslim refrains from food that is empty of God. It is, indeed, intensely physical. Yet it is this very physicality, this earthiness, that points the way to transcendence and God-consciousness.

As we have seen in this book, and throughout history, Islam has the power to initiate and sustain God-consciousness in persons and entire civilizations. And now Islam is with us in the United States and throughout the West—a jewel in our midst. It is a religion that brings each generation to a God-consciousness that fosters all that is human. Whether we are lay or religious, Christian or Muslim, we cannot afford to delegate this dialogue to specialists, academics, politicians, and military generals. We must bow our heads and bend our knees and, upon rising, extend our hands. We are friends.

CHAPTER SEVEN

A Response

⁌

SHAHID ATHAR, MD

Sister Mary Margaret Funk, a Catholic nun, has asked her Muslim friend and her interfaith dialogue partner to write this response to her book on Islam. As I started to write this, the TV screen was showing bombs falling on Baghdad and other cities in Iraq in a "shock and awe" campaign by the United States that some Muslims viewed as a war on Islam. Unfortunately, most Americans do not know that the former vice-president of Iraq, Tariq Aziz, is a Christian and that the former president and the ruthless dictator, Saddam Hussein, was a secular Muslim (if there is such a thing). He had gassed and killed thousands of fellow Muslims. Thus, this war is not as simple as some people may believe.

Sister Meg, as I call her, has much in common with me in addition to sharing One God. We have lived in the same town in the United States for several decades; we belong to the same interfaith movement and are dedicated to Muslim–Catholic dialogue. We are for peace and against war. She is both more saintly and more "normal" than I. (*Normal* is a term she uses for good Muslims.) We admire each other and communicate through e-mail on a regular basis. She calls me her brother and I call her my sister. We rarely see each other more than once a year. She is busy as a nun and I am busy as a physician. She invites people to God and I take care of their health. After the tragedy of September 11, 2001, a few hate-mongers sent me hate e-mail and a bomb threat. Sister Meg sent me a rose and a prayer of support.

Even though I believe that only those who live in a religion should speak for that religion, I see nothing wrong with anyone trying to understand and appreciate the theology of others and sharing it with those whose only source of education is television and print media. I especially support such attempts if they have a positive effect in removing some prevailing misconceptions and bring people of faith closer to each other for the love of a common God and loving service to fellow human beings, irrespective of their professed or assigned faith. In a lecture I gave at an international Sufi convention, I said that people of faith are like mountain climbers, trying to reach the same peak from different directions. I called them an army of God, wearing different uniforms but marching toward the same God—not a fighting army but a salvation army, in service to fellow humans.

Sister Meg's book on Islam comes at a time when, after the tragedy of September 11, there has been a wave of Islamophobia in the media, supported by some Christian evangelists. The Reverend Pat Robertson called Islam "the enemy," the Reverend Franklin Graham said Islam was "evil," the Reverend Jerry Falwell called the Prophet Muhammad a "terrorist" and the Qur'an "worse than *Mein Kampf*." The Reverend Jerry Vine from Florida called the Prophet Muhammad a "demon possessed" and a "pedophile." Sister Meg, however, calls Islam a jewel of religions and has high praise for the Prophet Muhammad. What a contrast of opinion among Christians! Meg is the kind of Christian that the Qur'an talks about when it says, "nearest in love, Muslims will find are those who call themselves Christians, as among them are those who are dedicated to learning, those who have renounced the material world [monastics], and those who are not arrogant" (Qur'an 5:32).

In writing some of my specific comments regarding the content of this book as a Muslim I do not intend to oppose or correct Meg's views, but to clarify the correct position of Islam on these views as I see them. For example, I disagree with Meg's notion that religion is crafted by humans. I believe that religion is inborn. The Qur'an states that when souls were

created, God took a pledge from them that they would
worship no God except one God or Allah, in Arabic
Ilahikumwahid ("our Lord is one"). This is also the
first commandment in the Bible, "Thou shall take no
partners to God." Thus, the Prophet Muhammad said,
"Children are born from nature (*fitra*) [submitting to
the will of God] but it is the parents who make them
Jews and Christians and people of other faiths." Thus,
I believe that all humans are believers, as religion was
built into them at the time of creation. Man is always
in search of God and is connected to God like a child
connected to mother via the umbilical cord. Those
who cannot find God create their own god in the form
of Marx, Lenin, or Stalin, unless they become their
own god, worshiping materialism and themselves.

The second question one may ask is, "Why were
different prophets sent? Wasn't Abraham alone
enough?" The problem in this question is that humans
rejected prophets during their lifetimes and persecuted
them. They even killed some of them. Those who
believed either forgot the teachings of their prophets
after their death or tried to distort them. Therefore,
we Muslims believe that Islam is not a new religion,
but it is the continuum of the same religion that was
revealed to Adam and to prophets through Jesus. The
Prophet Muhammad described himself as a beautiful
building, where people had noticed a missing block. If
this block was installed, they said, it would be

complete. The Prophet Muhammad said, "I am that missing block."

Muslims believe that Muhammad was foretold in the Bible and that Jesus knew about the coming of another prophet. For example, in John 14:16, New International Version, Jesus says, "And I will ask the Father, and he will give you another Counselor to be with you forever." And in Deuteronomy 18:18 it is mentioned, "I will raise up for them a prophet like you [Moses] from among their brothers; I will put my words in his mouth, and he will tell them everything I command him."

Muslims also believe that the events of the first revelation to Muhammad, described by Meg, were documented in the Bible as well. Isaiah 29:12 says, "Or if you give the scroll to someone who cannot read, and say, 'Read this, please,' he will answer, 'I don't know how to read.' "

I would also like to speak briefly about the status of Jesus and Mary in Islam. They are key to the unity of Christians and Muslims. Muslims love both of them and hold them in a very high position in our hearts. The miraculous conception and birth of Jesus is well described in the Qur'an Chapter 19, the chapter of Mary. Muslims believe that Jesus was born without a father as a sign from God. The Qur'an says that "the likeliness in the creation of Jesus is in the creation of Adam. He created him out of dust and

then He said unto him, 'Be and he is' " (3:59). I
jokingly say to my audiences sometimes that God at
least had one ingredient (i.e., a mother), in the
creation of Jesus, while in the creation of Adam he
had neither a mother nor a father. Muslims believe
that Jesus had many miracles given to him by God to
establish him as a prophet, which include the healing
of the blind and the leper, reviving the dead, and
making a bird out of clay. The Qur'an states that Jesus
did not die on the cross but was raised into the
heavens to be with God. Muslims are not waiting for
Muhammad or Moses to return but for Jesus to come
back to complete his mission.

Sister Meg describes beautifully her understanding
of the pillars of faith in Islam—belief, prayer, fasting,
charity, and pilgrimage. We know that no building is
composed of pillars only. It needs a floor, roof, walls,
windows, and so forth. These structures are the moral
codes of Islam—virtues such as honesty, truthfulness,
respect for parents and elders, kindness to neighbors,
love, and friendship. These values are common to all
religions, but are I believe especially shared by Islam
and Christianity. I would like to offer some specific
comments about the pillars.

Prayers: The formal prayers that are conducted
five times a day are called *salaat*. They are acts of
communication with God, not just asking God for our
needs. I am frequently asked why Muslims pray five

times a day. This is because, between prayers, worldly attractions instigated by Satan divert us from remembrance of God. Thus, we Muslims forget to practice the "presence of God" as Christians call it. In other words, the train of God-consciousness that derails must return to the track. We are closest to God when our forehead is touching the ground in prostration. Some Muslims may claim that their form of prayer is *the* Islamic prayer, but the fact is that it is the original prayer described in the Bible for all believers. It is mentioned in Nehemiah 8:6: "Ezra praised the Lord, the great God; and all the people lifted their hands and responded, 'Amen! Amen!' Then they bowed down and worshiped the Lord with their faces to the ground." Regarding Islamic prayer, another question that I get asked is why women have to pray behind men instead of in front of them or side by side. This is because our focus of attention must be God and nothing else. We do not pray behind any photographs or statues, either. However, within a house, a husband and wife can pray side by side.

Zakat or charity is the right of the poor over the wealth of the rich. Our modern tax system for welfare did not exist in the year 570 C.E., but evolved out of the *zakat* system developed by Islam.

Fasting in Ramadan is not new to Islam. It was prescribed by God to all religions in some form to clean the body and soul. It is a form of learning and

practicing self-restraint. As a physician, I can testify
that fasting has many medical benefits.

Hajj, the pilgrimage to Mecca, is not like a Disney
World tour. It combines all the rituals of Islam in the
tradition of Abraham. Having returned from my
second *hajj* to renew my faith, I cannot fully describe
the beauty, joy, and experience it offers. A Muslim is
reborn as sinless after performing a correct *hajj* and
considers it as a great honor to be called by God to
visit His first house, which we believe was built by
Adam. The *hajj* is something to be experienced rather
than described. How the *hajj* changes a person's spiritual growth, manifested in his external behavior, is
best described by Malcolm X in his conversion from a
hateful Muslim to a practicing true Muslim after
performing his *hajj*.

Finally, a word about terrorism. Islam teaches the
sanctity of life. Both in the Qur'an and in the Torah it
is mentioned that "if one kills one person, it is as if he
has killed all of mankind." However, terrorism is a
plague that now affects people of all faiths and of no
faith. Sometimes terrorism is intended by people to
defame their own faith. The terrorism committed by
extremists these days should be regarded as a hate
crime and not a religious act of piety. Sister Meg
mentions the example of Algerian monks killed by
Muslim terrorists. To my information, these monks
were killed not by Muslims, but by the secular

Algerian Army to defame the Islamic democratic movement in that country. Muslims, Christians, and people of other faiths must join hands to eradicate this disease from the hearts of hate-mongers by learning to love one other, and especially our "enemy"—as Jesus taught us in his Sermon on the Mount (Matthew 5:43–48).

It has been said, "Evil flourishes when few good folks don't do anything to oppose it." In the aftermath of September 11, 2001, interfaith dialogue, especially between Muslims and Christians, became a spiritual and essential tool in this war on terrorism. Those who want to see us fight will be very disappointed to see us unite as believers to promote religious harmony and world peace. I believe this book will open the minds and the hearts of Sister Meg's fellow Christians to Islam, and Muslims will thank her and say of her, "I wish she were a Muslim." Maybe she is and they don't know that Islam is not in name or in appearance but is a state of *islam* (submitting to the will of One God) in us.

CHAPTER EIGHT

The Mission of Muslim–Catholic Dialogue

≈

SHAHID ATHAR, MD

O mankind! We created you from a single (pair) of a male and female and made you into nations and tribes, that you may know each other (not that you may despise each other). Verily the most honored of you in the sight of Allah is (he who is) the most righteous of you. And Allah has full knowledge and is well acquainted (with all things). (Qur'an 49:13, translation by Abdullah Yusuf Ali)

Introduction

For the first eighteen years of my life, I lived in a small town in India and hardly had any contact with any Christians in that area. The next seven years of my life were spent in a metropolitan city in Pakistan, Karachi, where I studied medicine. There I had a few Christian friends in my class, but we never discussed

religion. When I arrived in Chicago in 1969, I knew
very little of my own religion. However, it became a
necessity for me to learn as well as to teach my children about my own faith and comparative religion in
order to have some working knowledge of the faith of
all those with whom I would interact. In 1984, and
seventeen years before 9/11, I saw the need for interfaith dialogue (when interfaith was considered a sin
by some Muslims). I became part of an interfaith
movement that was known in our city, Indianapolis,
as the North Side Interfaith Project. Subsequently, it
evolved into the Interfaith Alliance of Indianapolis. It
is now a vibrant organization, having fifty-six congregations of different faith traditions.

On October 22, 1996, we had the first Midwest
Muslim–Catholic dialogue in Indianapolis. I had the
pleasure of hosting it on behalf of Muslims, and
Father Tom Murphy of the Archdiocese of Indianapolis hosted it on behalf of Catholics. Catholic
bishops, imams, and other religious scholars from
Washington, DC, Chicago, New York, Louisville, St.
Louis, Toledo, Buffalo, Cleveland, Montana, and
Michigan attended. Our central point of discussion at
that time was entitled "Mary holds Muslims and
Christians in conversation." Each day of the two-day
conference the meeting started and ended with prayer,
and we also ate lunch and dinner together. Discussions
were held on both sides.

The second retreat, the following year, was again in Indianapolis, from October 14 to 15. At this gathering and for the next ten years, we discussed the word of God from a Catholic as well as an Islamic perspective. These discussions were published in a book entitled *Revelation: Catholic and Muslim Perspectives*, jointly published by The Islamic Society of North America as well as The United States Conference of Catholic Bishops. Many contributed to the discussion and to this valuable publication.

The Need for a Mission Statement

It is said that if you don't know where you are going, you will end up in a place where you never wanted to be. We Muslims and Catholics in leadership positions must know what our clear objective and mission are so we can relate them to our congregations. Christians and Muslims in the past 1,400 years have met on battlegrounds at times. We have also engaged in some personal debates but without much dialogue in an organized way.

As a physician, I must recognize the disease first and its signs and symptoms before I offer any treatment. Both Muslims and Christians who claim to have Abraham's faith believe in the Oneness of God and His manifestations. Sometimes, however, they live in apprehension about each other. Some Muslims may fear that Christian missionaries are out to occupy

and Christianize Muslim lands, and Christians fear
that Muslims are out to convert and enslave everyone
else by the sword. This apprehension—based on many
misconceptions—is the root of our misunderstandings, and results in verbal exchanges and writings that
cause each other hurt from time to time. It, therefore,
becomes a necessity for us to come to a dialogue of
understanding with each other.

Such a dialogue was routine in some of the enlightened past Muslim regimes in Baghdad and Spain;
however, it disappeared after the Crusades and the
Inquisition. The need reappeared in the latter part of
the last century with initiatives on both sides, but
especially from Pope John Paul II. After the tragedy of
9/11, it took a different direction. People of different
faiths, living in the United States, from fourteen
different religions as well as the governments in the
world, realized that we must enter into dialogue with
each other rather than provoke confrontations. There
have always been individual positive statements both
from the Muslims as well as the Christian/Catholic
leaders, but never as a group—until the tragedy of
9/11 brought us together.

*Our mission is to bring the masses together in
dialogue, not just the leadership.* However, what the
leadership agree on, and write and speak about, is not
being disseminated to their congregations. A common
joke in the media is that when a dog bites a man, it is

not news; but when a man bites a dog, it is. In a similar way, the more common activities of good works and words being disseminated by people of faith to promote religious harmony are not promoted; however, videos from Bin Laden and messages of hate catch the headlines. On September 22, 2007, the *Indianapolis Star* reported that a Christian priest in my hometown gave a sermon in which he questioned the loyalty of American Muslims. He called them an "open enemy planning to take over America." Several prominent people from both sides of the controversy responded to the accusations. This story demonstrates the urgent need for a mission statement with clear-cut guidelines for the future as well as for the laity.

What the Mission Is Not?
We must define what our mission is *not*. Some folks wrongly think of interfaith dialogue as mixing all faiths together and creating a new one. This is not true. What is also not true is that it is necessary to compromise one's own faith or give up part of it. Interfaith dialogue is not about who is right or who is wrong, whether "my God is bigger than your God" and "my God is going to beat up your God." Interfaith dialogue is about showing and talking and sharing one's faith with others, about sharing one's joys, sorrows, and celebrations with others. Interfaith dialogue is not accepting all or even part of the other

individual's faith on a theological basis; it is concerned with small gestures of kindness that are much appreciated and have an everlasting effect. For instance, it was very nice of Pope Benedict to visit Turkey and pray in the mosque with the Grand Mufti of Turkey. At the same time, his symbolic gesture to pray south, toward Mecca, was very much appreciated by Turkey's Muslims. This diminished the tension created by his previous (and misunderstood) statement about Islam and its prophet. Just as Pope Benedict visited the mosque, so I would encourage Muslims to visit churches and learn from some of the wisdom of the priests. I do it from time to time. One does not have to go to extremes to please others. It would be naïve of Christians to expect Muslims to start wearing crosses or believe in Jesus as the Son of God. By the same token, it would be naïve of Muslims to expect Christians to give up the divinity of Jesus or make ablution five times a day before praying. *It is not the mission of our dialogue to try to convert each other to our own faith. The conversion is done by God alone.*

Progress
Great progress has been made, both at individual as well as collective levels, by lay people as well as by leadership. I recall that in 1979, during the Iranian hostage crisis, Father Tom Murphy issued a statement, which said that American Muslims should not be

discriminated against or be faced with a backlash because of what happened in Iran. He also called to offer personal protection to me and my family should any crisis occur in our city—a very generous gesture. I considered the gesture to be an extension of the example of protection given by the Christian ruler of Abyssinia (Ethiopia) to the Muslim delegation of the Prophet's companions when they were seeking asylum from persecution by pagan Arabs. Similarly, during the civil war in Lebanon, as well as during the Palestinian Intifada, Muslims protected Christian groups.

Pope John Paul II and Pope Benedict have always issued greetings of peace to Muslims on Ramadan and Eid. Although Muslim leaders individually have also issued statements in support of Christians, we do not have a similar central authority. The weight of such statements, for example by the Islamic Society of North America, is not the same as that coming out from the Vatican. Most importantly, since 9/11 there has been a genuine desire from Christian congregations to invite Muslims to share their faith. The common quest for moral values, ethics, and spirituality between Catholics and Muslims has also brought us together. Personal friendships that have developed during these Muslim–Catholic dialogues have led to publications, such as this book, that have a far-reaching impact on both faith groups and have been well-received, not only by Catholics but also by

Muslims. Sister Meg also wrote and distributed 50,000 copies of her pamphlet "What Catholics Should Know about Islam." Muslim scholars need to write similar books about Christianity. Likewise, I believe that the book *Revelation: Catholic and Muslim Perspectives* should be publicized so it can reach all congregations on both sides. For some reason, Muslims are less aware of the presence of this book than are Catholics. It would be nice that when churches are threatened in a Muslim country, Muslims would come out and befriend and protect those churches rather than be bystanders. If we treat others and their children as our own children, then the world would be a better place in which to live.

Responsibility

What is the role of the faith community in uplifting and relieving the suffering of humanity in general, and Americans in particular?

I believe that taking care of fellow humans and all other creations of God becomes our collective responsibility, whether we like it or not. The sufferings of human beings—homelessness, poverty, drug addiction, natural catastrophes—are not only the will of God, but a test from Him of how we patiently persevere and do our best to relieve those who are suffering.

The social obligations of believers include taking care of those who have not, irrespective of their faith.

There are about twenty million people who live below the poverty level—forty percent of whom are children. The responsibilities of people of faith include the establishment of shelters, halfway houses for runaway teenagers, rehabilitation for drug addicts, combating violence on the streets, and fighting discrimination and racism. The responsibilities of those who leave houses of worship after their prayers consist of going on to the streets and introducing love within their families, neighborhoods, the community, and among the religions.

As we travel spiritually through the next millennium, we must forget and forgive our differences and give some gifts to our fellow humans and Mother Earth. Our talk of peace for this millennium should be followed by peaceful actions, such as human rights for all, gender equality, the right to earn a living and have basic needs satisfied, as well as ending hostility based on religion, language, and ethnicity.

We must develop programs to implement these goals in our communities, joining with other forces in the same cause. We must do all this for the pleasure of the same God whom we like to visit in our prayers.

The Future

Interfaith work needs to be directed toward creating a better and more tolerant environment in a pluralistic society. Its main purpose is to create mutual understanding among people of different faiths so that cooperation on future agreed-upon goals and peaceful existence becomes possible.

1) We must accept that everyone has a right to choose his or her own beliefs and religion. "Let there be no compulsion in religion" (Qur'an 2:256).

2) We must show respect for others' beliefs without having to agree with those beliefs.

3) We may want to share our own beliefs with others when asked about them.

4) We must do our best to remove misconceptions about our beliefs in the minds of others and the beliefs of others in our minds.

5) We should seek a common ground in beliefs expressed in actions that take care of the society we both live in—whether it is homelessness, poverty, drug addiction, etc. Believers are joined together in performing good deeds in their societies and in expressing concern about, and condemning, the bad things that happen—such as violence. As the Qur'an says, "Let among you arise a party of believers who invite others to do good and forbid what is wrong."

Interfaith work has a certain etiquette and set of manners that can be summarized in the following dos and don'ts:

1) Don't be judgmental of others; as the Bible says, "Judge not and you shall not be judged" and the Qu'ran (95:8), "Is not God greatest of all Judges?"
2) Do not proclaim "Only I will go to heaven, therefore you must join me in my religion if you want to be saved."
3) One does not need to compromise or give up part of one's faith. One also does not have to say that all other religions are correct or they are wrong at the same time, for this is up to God to decide.

We should have an open discussion on these points and develop a concise statement on the points on which we agree. Whatever we agree should be presented to other clergy as well as the masses. Then, we should have a target-practice session and evaluation. Instead of living in our own closets, we should get out and visit each other's homes, places of work and worship, as well as their hearts. During any crisis in the community, nationally, or internationally, we must stand by each other with full support—whether that crisis is political or natural, such as with a hurricane, tsunami, or earthquake. Our leaders should choose their words very carefully before they speak or write because, while they may have good intentions, they may be misreported in the media and misunderstood by the masses, and so cause damage.

The challenge between our faiths is not a war between Islam and Christianity. We have bigger enemies to fight. We must show our unity together as believers, otherwise disbelief, materialism, and secularism will take over. Our mission is to unite with each other, not necessarily on a theological level but on a human level for the betterment of our future generations.

One hundred and thirty-eight Muslim scholars around the world from all schools of thought who wrote to Pope Benedict XVI and other Christian leaders in 2007 urging them to help bring about greater understanding. They noted that the world's future depended on peace between the two faiths.

On page 49 of *Revelation: Catholic and Muslim Perspectives* it says:

We would like to stress how much Catholics and Muslims share belief in One God, Who created the universe and all it contains, out of love; the conviction that the center of religious life is surrender and obedience to the will of God; and the confidence that God's will is a transforming power that can renew individual and social life in every aspect. Through dialogue and improved cooperation, Muslims and Catholics can develop a just and peaceful society in the spirit of the teachings of the Gospel and Qur'an. Both Jesus and Mohammad loved and cared for all whom they met, especially the poor and oppressed; their teachings and examples call for solidarity with the poor, oppressed, homeless, hungry, and needy in today's world (irrespective of their faith or no faith as God feeds them all).

At the end of the latest two-day conference, Catholic Bishops, Muslim imams, and scholars from both religions drafted and agreed upon the following statement:

Catholics and Muslims engage in interreligious dialogue because it is part of our core identities as people of faith. Our common belief in One God of Mercy and Love calls us into relationship with one another. We view dialogue as a spiritual journey.

This chapter is adapted from a presentation given on October 22, 2007, in Dearborn, Michigan, during the Eleventh Conference on Midwest Muslim–Catholic Dialogue.

CHAPTER NINE

What Would Thomas Merton Do?

⌒

At a family gathering a few years ago there was intense talk about the current Iraq War and upcoming elections. Like most families, mine is sharply divided. The range of opinion is not unusual. It's also normal to have many points of view and to hear vastly different sides in a debate. What was striking this time was the level of intensity, the sustained informed narrative brought to the table, and the despair at finding common ground. It was my fifteenth year of being involved with monastic interreligious dialogue and my eleventh year of having it as my full-time assignment. Isn't there some skillfulness we can bring to a family gathering from our experience? Or do we dialogue "out there" but remain mute in our home monastic communities and family reunions?

At one point I dropped out of the conversation and became an observer, asking myself some questions: I wonder what Thomas Merton would have said about our contemporary dilemma? Would

terrorism justify laying aside a nonviolent strategy?
Would Thomas Merton have grown up and out of the
1960s mentality that was so optimistic? We, who were
already adults in the 1960s, actually thought that war
would become obsolete. Forty years later there seems
to be no prospect for finding solutions other than
military ones. More disturbing is the fact that the
reliance on nonviolence as an alternative seems to fuel
more opposition and actually causes aggression
instead of promoting peace.

Conjectures of a Guilty Bystander

So, what would Merton do? In an interview published
in Issue 74 of the Monastic Interreligious Dialogue
bulletin, Brother Patrick Hart recommended *Conjectures of a Guilty Bystander* as a vintage model of
Merton's writing and style of engaged dialogue. In this
classic book, first published by Doubleday in 1966,
and from the second edition (1968) of which all the
following quotations are taken, we get not only a
glimpse of Merton's finest thinking and writing but
also a voice for monastics to imitate.

Merton said that the book was about a decade of
"personal reflections, insights, metaphors, observations, judgments on readings and events" (Preface),
and that in the book he would present his "version of
the world." The genius of Merton was that he *had* a
version of the world—that is, he could step back and

look and then articulate it both for himself and for others, like us. In other words, he put this version "out there" and thereby began and sustained a dialogue with the world. We may not have his immense capacity to receive and interpret the world with his brilliant mind, excellent education, and universal contacts with the intellectual and artistic community of the 1960s; but we can notice what he did and how he did it, and imitate his "doing" of dialogue "in the world."

Merton's fundamental belief was that being a monk, rather than disqualifying him from having a point of view, gave him a vantage point that offered a unique and universal perspective. As a human, he was engaged in living in our actual world. He says of *Conjectures*:

Maybe the best way to characterize this book is to say that it consists of a series of sketches and meditations, some poetic and literary, others historical and even theological, fitted together in a spontaneous, informal philosophic scheme in such a way that they react upon each other. The total result is a personal and monastic meditation, a testimony of Christian reflection in the mid-twentieth century, a confrontation of twentieth-century questions in the light of monastic commitment,

which inevitably makes one something of a
"bystander." (Preface, pp. v–vi)

A Voice for Praise and Worship

Merton then proceeds to move through contemporary
news items, philosophical systems, poetry, theology,
and all manner of things in a way that makes an op-
ed page look one-dimensional. In scanning this book
for the sake of my dialogue practice, I read with the
intention of understanding just what the "voice" of a
bystander is. What did Merton see that I wanted to
notice for myself? At one point near the end of
Conjectures, Merton portrays a particular day on
retreat:

> We are on retreat. Very cold morning, about 8
> degrees above. I left for the woods before
> dawn, after a conference on sin. Pure dark sky,
> with only the crescent moon and planets
> shining: the moon and Venus over the barns,
> and Mars in the west over the hills and the fire
> tower.
>   Sunrise is an event that calls forth solemn
> music in the very depths of man's nature, as if
> one's whole being had to attune itself to the
> cosmos and praise God for the new day, praise
> Him in the name of all the creatures that ever
> were or ever will be. I look at the rising sun and

feel that now upon me falls the responsibility of seeing what all my ancestors have seen, in the Stone Age and even before it, praising God before me. Whether or not they praised Him, then, for themselves, they must praise Him now in me. When the sun rises, each one of us is summoned by the living and the dead to praise God. (p. 280)

The authority that all contemplatives, lay, and monastics claim is that we come from the cloister of solitude. "You must be free, and not involved," writes Merton. "Solitude is to be preserved, not as a luxury but as a necessity: not for 'perfection' so much as for simple 'survival' in the life God has given you" (p. 97).

It's in this solitude we name the contemplative moment from our ongoing practice of *lectio divina*. Our eyes are trained to "see."

I pray much to have a wise heart, and perhaps the rediscovery of Lady Julian of Norwich will help me. I took her book with me on a quiet wall among the cedars. . . . She really elaborates, theologically, the content of her revelations. She first experienced, then thought, and the thoughtful deepening of experience worked its way back into her life, deeper and deeper, until her whole life as a recluse at Norwich was simply a matter of getting completely saturated in the light she had received all at once, in the "shewings," when she thought she was about to die. . . . To have a "wise heart," it seems to me [continues Merton, commenting about Julian of Norwich], is to live centered on this dynamism and this secret hope—this hoped-for secret. It is the key to our life; but as long as we are alive we must see that we do not have this key: it is not at our disposal. Christ has it, in us, for us. We have the key in so far as we believe in Him, and are one with Him. So this is it: the "wise heart" remains in hope and in contradiction, in sorrow and in joy, fixed on the secret and the "great deed" which alone gives Christian life its true scope and dimensions!

The wise heart lives in Christ. (p. 212)

Two words from the title of his book—"guilty" and "bystander"—function as an idiom of watching, from the outside. We monastics often use the collective, personal pronoun "we" as a way of accepting responsibility for the current condition and for expressing our joint commitment to accountability for the next generation, to taking action on behalf of those who will follow us. The "we" of Thomas

Merton's writings is saturated with compassion and hope. However, this collective "we" is only half of the monastic's vocation in the world. Merton uses the singular "I" when he names the *now* of each contemplative moment. Notice the passage above: "We are on retreat." "I look at the rising sun." We might share our concerns about America at war, but to miss the *now* that is calling for praise and worship would mean forsaking an important part of our vocation.

A Voice for Protest and Honest Talk
However, Merton also knew that monastics cannot limit their activity to praise and worship. He once said that he wanted to make his entire life a protest against the injustice and cruelty that are as evident in our world today as when he was writing forty or more years ago. We simply must ask, "Why war?"— a question I have asked of some of my relatives. I believe the following lines from Merton do much to explain our ongoing Iraq War:

> The basic falsehood is the lie that we are totally dedicated to truth, and that we can remain dedicated to truth in a manner that is at the same time honest and exclusive: that we have a monopoly of all truth, just as our adversary of the moment has the monopoly of all error. We then convince ourselves that we

cannot preserve our purity of vision and our
inner sincerity if we enter into dialogue with
the enemy, for he will corrupt us with his error.
We believe, finally, that truth cannot be
preserved except by the destruction of the
enemy—for, since we have identified him with
error, to destroy him is to destroy error. The
adversary, of course, has exactly the same
thoughts about us and exactly the same as our
policy, by which he defends the "truth." He
has identified us with dishonesty, insincerity,
and untruth. He believes that, if we are
destroyed, nothing will be left but truth. (p. 68)

Why do we need to prove our enemy wrong?
"Because," Merton writes, "we need them to be
wrong." He continues:

For if they are wrong, and we are right, then
our untruth becomes truth: our selfishness
becomes justice and virtue: our cruelty and lust
cannot be fairly condemned. We can rest secure
in the fiction we have determined to embrace
as "truth." What we desire is not the truth, but
rather that our lie should be proved "right,"
and our iniquity be vindicated as "just." This is
what we have done to pervert our natural,
instinctive appetite for truth. (p. 78)

Truth itself can be a trick. When we have "the truth," this gives us permission to hate. Merton gives an example drawn from table reading at his monastery:

> In the refectory a tendentious book about Communism is being read. Communism is insidious. We should hate all that is insidious, especially this ultimate diabolical insidiousness which is Communism. If we truly hate it with all the power of our being, then we can be sure we ourselves are, and will remain, righteous, free, sincere, honest, open. Today then (we are told) hatred of Communism is the test of a good Christian. The pledge of all truth is our political hate. Hate Castro. Hate Khrushchev. Hate Mao. All this in the same breath as "God's merciful love" and the "beatings of the Sacred Heart." There seems to be some other dimension we have not discovered. (p. 44)

Merton even cautions the monastic about positing another "truth" that trumps the previous abuse of truth. His skillful method toward love that informs and forms truth is this: "The best I can do is to look for some of the questions" (p. 49). So, I guess Merton would not have appeared on a talk show. Being a monk he could stand back and watch. But his genius was to watch without being hooked into the crisis. He also insisted on the importance of thought, of being a thinking person:

> Nothing can take the place of thoughts. If we do not think, we cannot act freely. If we do not act freely, we are at the mercy of forces which we never understand, forces that are arbitrary, destructive, blind, fatal to us and to our world. If we do not use our minds to think with, we are heading for extinction, like the dinosaur: for the massive physical strength of the dinosaur became useless, purposeless. It led to his destruction. (p. 79)

Personal Lessons

Having reviewed some of the most potent teachings in *Conjectures*—and nothing substitutes for the direct experience of doing it leisurely yourself—let me continue by reflecting on some ways in which Merton's book might serve as a tool for me the next time I'm at the Funk family table and the political world becomes part of the menu, no matter what the feast.

First, I must continue to do my own practice so as not to participate unconsciously as a person of the lie and claim to "see" the hidden agenda of others from my own store of hubris. My own anger, competition, and propensity to retaliate and maintain the cycle of violence needs to be rooted out with practice before coming to the dinner table and to the table of dialogue. I fear not only "the Lord" but also my own stored tendencies to "kill my enemies," even if they are my kindred by blood or ties of friendship.

I don't apologize for being a nun and bringing to the table views that I have picked up from here, from there, from reading, from other conversations—views that are neither better than nor richer than others, but just "other views." Being in this world and actually living today is the only warrant to engage in the conversation. However, silence, when not used passive-aggressively, is my greatest strength before, during, and after the talk.

I would bring to the table that contemplative "eye of the heart" that has the witness of the "we" but the urgency rising from the "I." The description of Merton's night watch when he was Novice Master serves as an ode to all of us who see: "Looking at the dark empty room, with everyone gone, it seemed that, because all that they loved was there, 'they' in a spiritual way were most truly there, though in fact they were all upstairs in the dormitory, asleep."

Merton goes on to reflect:

It was as if their love and their goodness had transformed the room and filled it with a presence curiously real, comforting, perfect: one might say, with Christ. Indeed, it seemed to me

momentarily that He was as truly present here,
in a certain way, as upstairs in the Chapel. The
loveliness of the humanity which God has
taken to Himself in love is, after all, to be seen
in the humanity of friends, our children, our
brothers, the people we love and who love us.
Now that God has become Incarnate, why do
we go to such lengths, all the time, to "disin-
carnate" Him again, to unweave the garment
of flesh and reduce Him once again to spirit?
As if the Body of the Lord had not become
"Life-giving Spirit." . . .

In any case, I felt there was something quite
final and eternal in looking at this empty room:
. . . how precious. It is very good to have loved
and been loved by them with such simplicity
and sincerity." (p. 214)

Most of all, what contemplatives bring to the table
of dialogue is to gently raise up in the midst of disso-
nance the contemplative moment of the here and now.
I'm here at this table, belonging to this family and
coming from my particular monastery. Merton has the
words to describe this attitude:

Dealing with these brothers, my attitude
toward the monastery changes. I see that they
have need of me, and I have need of them, and

I am glad to do what I can for them. This is a source of peace that makes much more sense than aiming at something less attainable and then being dissatisfied because one has not "attained" it. (p. 280)

So, stay at the table.

A View and a Voice

So what would Merton do? Perhaps he'd say we need a view, a voice, and a vocation.

No one really wants your "view" at the table of dialogue. Different views seem to aggravate rather than lift up the conversation to the noble, the insightful, or the compassionate action. There's an edge to one's view. It often lacks maturity. Views often become polarities and create an oppositional climate rather than move the conversation to harmony, peace, and community. There's another level that must be cultivated by each individual and by groups that are preparing to come to the table of dialogue: *a voice.* We need to be clear, compelling, authentic, seasoned, and appropriate. Our voice, not our view, has the capacity to mediate truth. Views solicit opposing views and reactions rather than wisdom. Voice invites pause, wonder, and response. Views debate and divide: voice discerns and bonds.

What would our "voice" look like? From the

outside the voice would be speaking in the first person. The speaker takes responsibility and comes from his or her center. The speaker's voice is personal and, while speaking from the "I," it's not the "I" of the ego, but the "I" that offers a relationship to the "you" (the *du* of which Martin Buber speaks). This voice refrains from speaking at someone or resorting to *principles* rather than sharing from the heart *personal* convictions that are born of an experience of silence. The voice comes from the center of the "I." The ego is muted. Excluded from our voice would be words of power and control, competition and dominance, seduction and intrusion, moralism or dogmatism that drive arguments and score points. Dialogue is not debate, no matter how skillful. Nor is dialogue rhetoric. No amount of style compensates for substance. The voice is humble and creates spaciousness. Poised pauses honor distinctions; differences contrast preferences; subtleties foster appreciation.

This voice welcomes differences, because distinctions do not divide but enhance the beauty with contrast and subtlety that foster unity. You might wonder about the "what if" you don't agree with, or if the "other" is ignorant or even harmful if taken to conclusions. Negativity, no matter its many disguises, has no place at the table of dialogue. *Negate nothing*, say the ancients. *What is, is.*

Dialogue is bigger than any person at the table. No

one needs to defend truth. With humility, wisdom and charity emerge as a shared experience. Yet here is where the view comes in again through the back door. A formed view makes a contribution beyond opinion, ego, and reaction. There is no substitute for homework. Here's a list of some of Merton's *views* that were responses to the use of war as a means of peace:

- Merton did not accept St. Augustine's just war theory, which taught that it is possible to kill others morally if one intends objectives other than the killing and if war is the last resort. Merton said that the divorce between intention and behavior creates a moral schizophrenia in which one's motives are separated from one's actions, in this case, killing a human being. It was Augustine's way of thinking that permitted the Crusades and the Inquisition.

- Merton espoused Gandhi's nonviolence, which seeks to liberate the adversary from the mentality that makes violence and oppression appealing. Since there is no separation between the oppressor and the oppressed, there is no enemy.

- Merton raised up the imperative of nonviolence in the early Church tradition. Clement of Alexandria observed that a disciple of Christ is a soldier of peace in an army that sheds no blood. St. Justin concluded that a Christian does not take another's life but dies for Christ. Tertullian, with his striking way of writing, insisted that Jesus disarmed every Christian soldier when he told Peter to put away his sword.

- Nonviolence imposes the need to root out our fascination for total solutions to problems and totalitarian approaches to life. We become violent because we believe we alone have the answers and the truth. We conclude that any alternative to our position must make matters worse and be false. There is arrogance in this.

- Christians become belligerent, Merton affirmed, because they see the truth as smaller than they are, as something less significant than the Church. No, Merton thundered. The truth is larger than we are. It endures even when we do not defend it. We are not the possessors of truth but its servants. The truth is more than we are, more than the Church is. The Church is a minister to the truth, a witness to it, not its master.

- If we believe that the truth is invincible, then we do not attack others to preserve it. Those who genuinely serve the truth are gentle with it and humble. The truth need only be spoken and its force can be felt. When we defend the so-called truth by violence, we are not serving the truth but ourselves. We turn to violence because we are aware at some level of consciousness that the truth is not in us and we are, therefore, insecure with what we propose as the truth.

- Those we define as our enemies are often not our enemies but simply those we cannot control, those who take options in life we did not, those who see an aspect of the truth to which we are blind. This is not to assume that there are no wicked people in the world; it is merely to state that there are far fewer than we suspect. Many of those we declare wicked are not wicked, but different.

- Fear is the root cause of war. With bigger and bigger weapons we will continue to dominate and be dominated.

- Nonviolence requires spiritual maturity. This is why prayer is an important element in the achievement of nonviolence. The reason why nonviolence fails to work on many occasions is because others sense correctly that beneath the surface of the nonviolence there is a hidden belligerence, a desire to control or, at the very least, an assumption of moral superiority and self-righteousness.

- Nonviolence is a humble approach to life, seeking to purify the self from the vanity that gets in the way of our happiness and the greed that makes us violent with one another.

- Two assumptions by those who advocate violence are: that I am separate from the other, and that I can hurt the other without injuring myself.

Violence seems advantageous: if I don't guard my interests, another will take them. Scarcity thus dictates a felt need to protect American interests.[1]

Vocation

So, you might ask, exactly just what homework is necessary to form a view? And where does one find a *voice*? This is another way of saying that the view must rise through a trained voice. Most people move quickly to share their educated view and miss the dynamics of dialogue.

Our voice rises from our vocation: As praying people we follow the calling to be Christ for others. If we use the image of a river, we are viewed from what people see and our interior life is hidden or spiritual. Above the river we look ordinary and wear clothing of nothing special; but under the river we are practitioners of prayer and sustained self-discipline. When we have trained in ascetical life (inner work) the ego relaxes its grip and from underneath Wisdom herself rises and we surrender to her voice. We can speak with a voice, the voice of a contemplative that transcends the oppositional polarities and speaks heart to heart.

Let me be more specific: Recognize the five warning signs:

- Stereotyping opposing positions: e.g., liberal vs. conservative, or nonviolence vs. mili-

tarism, stances that freeze options and para-
lyze skillful actions
- Dealing in abstractions (-isms or -ologies)
that polarize and totalize strategies
- Undervaluing the personal and the rela-
tional, and thereby fostering an attitude of
"us vs. enemies"
- Hiding behind ego-centered resistance and
defensiveness that is fear-based
- Resorting to negativity and dichotomies
that narrow the field of vision

Five innovative dialogue skills and practices:

- Speaking in the first person
- Shifting from ideologies to persons
- Shifting from truth as an abstraction to
personal beliefs, hopes, and experiences of
the sacred
- Shifting from ego-centered resistance to a
shared consciousness of the sacred and of
the human
- Shifting from negativity to a conscious willingness to understand and honor differences

Practices before and during Dialogue

- Prepare for dialogue with a week of prayer
and moderate fasting.

- Have an ascetical practice that purifies your thoughts and emotions so that your own afflictions are not hindrances at the table of dialogue.
- Have methods of laying aside one's personal afflictions of anger and dejection so that one is aware of the thoughts that rise unconsciously at the table of dialogue. (This teaching would draw on John Cassian's treatment of "the eight thoughts": food, sex, things, anger, dejection, acedia, vainglory, and pride.)[2]
- Find a personal prayer practice that is ceaseless and that creates a place of refuge where one finds peace and an inner emptiness to receive another.
- Wait upon the Spirit, who teaches us when, how, to whom, and what to say. (This would include such prayer practices as the Jesus Prayer, Abandonment to the Present Moment, The Little Way, Colloquy, and Emptiness.)[3]
- Embrace *lectio divina* as the integrating prayer form for each contemplative practitioner to put on the mind of Jesus Christ as our formation for dialogue.

The ancient desert tradition teaches that, with

God's grace, affliction is taken away and replaced with prayer. Continuous prayer awakens the practitioner to Presence, the shared place of Being and Essence.

A vocation is not achieved. We follow our calling to be steeped in Christ Consciousness. The directives that rise from underneath our mindless free-falling thoughts and move toward the gentle stirrings of the Holy Spirit take us from light to light, insight to insight. We might find ourselves in unlikely places. In humility we sit in silence and have an inner knowing of the heart. Our voice is the contemplative silence punctuated by a word.

Merton, in his *Conjectures of a Guilty Bystander*, did two things: he named the situation with clarity and artistic soundness, and he also used the voice of "we" accepting the full burden of the human condition. His writings came from his informed view, but his voice was from his contemplative way of life. He tasted humility and knew from experience the "we" of existence.

The ancient desert tradition teaches that with God's grace affliction is taken away and replaced with prayer. Continuous prayer awakens the practitioner to Presence, the shared place of Being and Essence. This is the ultimate zone of dialogue. This point, however, needs to be stressed: That one's experience is about the other and not the self-referencing ego. The vocation of the one who prays at the table of dialogue is to give voice to Christ mediated through our own knowing and being known.

As mystical as this might sound, there is no other way to meet and mediate the complexities of our times. We pray. Sincere prayer leads us to due diligence and discipline of doing our homework on our view—war, immigration, globalization, pandemics, distribution of resources: the list is endless. We give attention to our vocation that calls us to prayer and to ascetical work that removes the inner obstacles to prayer. Finally, our inner attention directs our voice as to when we speak, to whom, with whom, and what to say. We literally get out of the way so that God speaks through us and we listen with the ear of our heart. Thomas Merton today would smile because we no longer should have need to quote him, or any other prophet; but to be there and speaking as one having authority, possessing an inner confidence that during our lifetime Peace is possible.

NOTES

⌒

Chapter One

1. Our Lady of Grace Monastery was founded in 1961 in Ferdinand, Indiana. This Benedictine Monastery has eighty-five nuns and sponsors St. Paul Hermitage, a retirement facility for lay elderly, and Benedict Inn, a retreat and Conference Center. The monastery is now located in Beech Grove, near Indianapolis. Our Lady of Grace Monastery can be contacted via the Web, at www.benedictine.com, or email: olgmonastery@aol.com.

2. MID was established in 1978 at the request of the Congress of Abbots and is accountable to the Vatican's Pontifical Council of Interreligious Dialogue under the General Secretary Pierre de Bethune of MID and its European branch, DIM. Its website, www.monastic-dialog.com, provides extensive coverage of its current work and previous accomplishments.

Chapter Two

1. James Harpur, *The Atlas of Sacred Places: Meeting Points of Heaven and Earth* (New York: Henry Holt & Co., 1994), pp. 208–9.

2. Quoted in *The Benefactor* by Fakir Syed Waheeduddin (Chicago: Kazi Publications, 1961).
3. "Muhammad." *Encyclopædia Britannica* 2003. www.britannica.com/eb/article?eu=108142, viewed December 28, 2007.

Chapter Five

1. In "Religion and Satanism," dated April 10, 2002. The Chalcedon Foundation.
2. Armand Veilleux, personal correspondence, Sunday, March 9, 2003.
3. "Status of Woman in Islam," Islamic Circle of North America. This little flyer consolidates current teachings on the issue. It is available from ICNA, 166-26 89th Avenue, Jamaica, NY 11432, Tel.: 1-718-658-1198 or 1-800-662-ISLAM. The pamphlet shows the Prophet's openness to women for his times and carries forward the most wholesome directions of this most sensitive human issue.
4. See the Gethsemani Encounter II at www.monasticdialog.com.
5. 2002. Available from the International Institute of Islamic Thought, PO Box 669, Herndon, VA 20172-0669.

Chapter Nine

1. The original list was gleaned from Anthony Padovano's book, *A Retreat with Thomas Merton: Becoming Who We Are* (Cincinnati: St. Anthony Press, 1995, pp. 73–75). A longer version of this chapter can be found

in the Monastic Interreligious Dialogue bulletins, numbers 73 and 74, available at www.monasticdialog.com.

2. As discussed in my book *Thoughts Matter*, published by Continuum in 1999.

3. As discussed in my book *Tools Matter*, published by Continuum in 2001.

BIBLIOGRAPHY

Armstrong, Karen. *Islam: A Short History*. Rev. ed. (New York: Modern Library, 2002).

———. *Muhammad: A Biography of the Prophet* (San Francisco: HarperCollins, 1992).

Athar, Shahid. *Reflections of an American Muslim* (Chicago: Kazi Publications, 1994).

Baker, Rob, and Gray Henry (eds.). *Merton and Sufism: The Untold Story* (Louisville, Ky.: Fons Vitae, 1999).

Ernst, Carl W., PhD. *Sufism: An Essential Introduction to the Philosophy and Practice of the Mystical Tradition of Islam* (Boston, London: Shambhala, 1997).

Fisher, Norman, Yifa, Judith Simmer-Brown, and Joseph Goldstein. *Benedict's Dharma: Buddhists Reflect on the Rule of St. Benedict* (New York: Riverhead, 2001).

Hathout, Hassan. *Reading the Muslim Mind* (Burr Ridge, Ill.: American Trust Publications, 1995).

His Holiness the Dalai Lama. *Spiritual Advice for Buddhists and Christians* (New York: Continuum, 1998).

Islam: The Story of Islam. A History of the World's Most Misunderstood Faith (MPI. Home Video, 1990).

Kaltner, John. *What Non-Muslims Should Know* (Minneapolis: Fortress Press, 2003).

Lewis, Bernard. "I'm Right, You're Wrong, Go to Hell." *Atlantic Monthly*, Vol. 291, No. 4, May 2003, p. 39.

Merton, Thomas. *Conjectures of a Guilty Bystander* (New York: Image, 1968).

Miles-Yepez, Netanel (ed.). *The Common Heart: An Experience of Interreligious Dialogue* (New York: Lantern Books, 2006).

Mitchell, Donald W., and James Wiseman (eds.). *The Gethsemani Encounter: A Dialogue on the Spiritual Life by Buddhist and Christian Monastics* (New York: Continuum, 1997).

———. *Transforming Suffering: Reflections on Finding Peace in Troubled Times* (New York: Doubleday, 2003).

Noss, David S. *A History of the World's Religions*, Tenth Edition (Upper Saddle River, N.J.: Simon & Schuster, 1994).

Schimmel, Annemarie. *My Soul Is a Woman: The Feminine in Islam* (New York: Continuum, 1994).

The Meaning of the Glorious Koran: An Explanatory Translation. Trans. Mohammed Marmaduke Pickthall (Multan, Pakistan: Maktaba Jawahar al Uloom, n.d.).

Tweedie, Irina. *The Chasm of Fire*. 1979. (Rockport, Mass.: Element, 1993).

William Skudlarek, OSB. "Zazen: From Judgment to Love," in *Purity of Heart and Contemplation*, Bruno Barnhart and Joseph Wong (eds.).

Veilleux, Armand. Personal correspondence, Sunday, March 9, 2003.

Wong, Joseph, and Bruno Barnhart (eds.). *Purity of Heart and Contemplation: A Monastic Dialogue between Christian and Asian Traditions* (New York: Continuum, 2002).

Yifa. *Safeguarding the Heart: A Buddhist Response to Suffering and September 11* (New York: Lantern Books, 2002).

Websites

Gethsemani Abbey: www.monks.org

Meg Funk: www.megfunk.com

Monastic Interreligious Dialogue: www.monasticdialog.com

The Thomas Merton Center: www.merton.org

CONTRIBUTORS

~

Shahid Athar, MD, FACE, FACP, is a physician who has practiced Endocrinology at St. Vincent Hospital, Indianapolis, since 1974. He is a Fellow, American College of Physicians and American College of Endocrinology, and a Clinical Associate Professor of Medicine at Indiana University School of Medicine in Indianapolis. He is a United States citizen and lives in Indianapolis with his wife. They have four children. His most recent book is *Healing the Wounds of September 11, 2001* (Authorhouse). His other books are *Reflections of an American Muslim, Health Concerns for Believers* and *Sex Education: An Islamic Perspective* (Kazi). His books and writings can be accessed on the Internet at www.islam-usa.com. Dr. Athar is the recipient of the 2007 Laureate award from American College of Physicians (Indiana chapter).

John Borelli, PhD, is a Special Assistant to the President of Georgetown University. In that position, he promotes ecumenical and interreligious initiatives and also serves as the National Coordinator for Interreligious Dialogue for the U.S. Jesuit Conference. Recently, Archbishop Michael

L. Fitzgerald and he have published *Interfaith Dialogue: A Catholic View.* For over sixteen years, he was Associate Director for the Secretariat for Ecumenical and Interreligious Affairs at the U.S. Conference of Catholic Bishops, and was a consultor to the Vatican's Pontifical Council for Interreligious Dialogue for seventeen years. He and his wife, Marianne, have been married for thirty-seven years. They have three children and a grandson. Before moving to Washington, DC, in 1987, they lived in New York for sixteen years, each earning a doctorate and beginning their careers in higher education. Marianne is a psychiatric mental health clinician and an adult primary care nurse practitioner.

Archbishop Michael L. Fitzgerald was President of the Pontifical Commission for Interreligious Dialogue from 2002 to 2006, and now serves as Apostolic Nuncio to the Arab Republic of Egypt and Delegate to the Organization of the League of Arab States.

BOOKS BY MARY MARGARET FUNK

Humility Matters
The Practice of the Spiritual Life

Thoughts Matter
The Practice of the Spiritual Life

Tools Matter for Practicing the Spiritual Life

El Corazón En Paz
La Sabiduria De Los Padres Del Desierto